Boats in the Desert

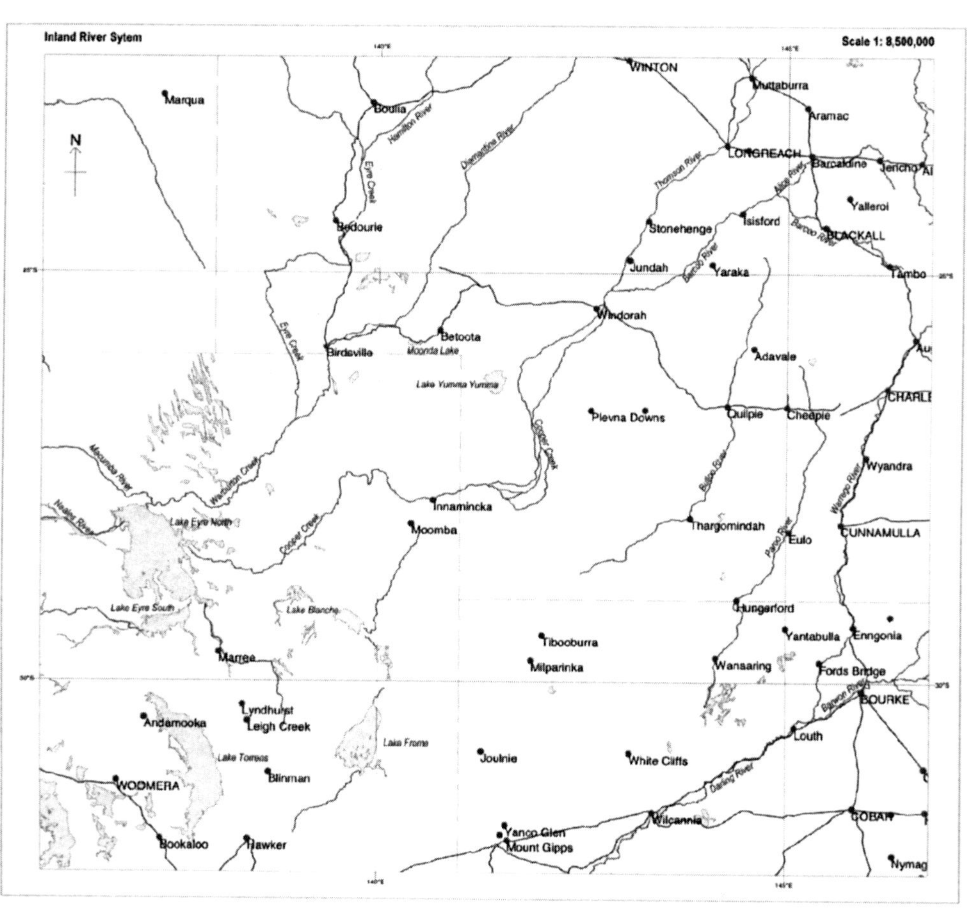

Inland River Sytem
Scale 1: 8,500,000
N
140°E
145°E
25°S
30°S
Marqua
Boulia
Hamilton River
Diamantina River
Eyre Creek
Bedourie
WINTON
Muttaburra
Aramac
LONGREACH
Barcaldine
Jericho
Thomson River
Alice River
Yalleroi
Stonehenge
Isisford
Barcoo River
BLACKALL
Jundah
Yaraka
Tambo
Windorah
Betoota
Moonda Lake
Birdsville
Adavale
Lake Yumma Yumma
Plevna Downs
Quilpie
Cheepie
Cooper Creek
Macumba River
Warburton Creek
Neales River
Lake Eyre North
Innamincka
Moomba
Wyandra
Warrego River
Bulloo River
Thargomindah
Paroo River
Eulo
CUNNAMULLA
Lake Eyre South
Lake Blanche
Hungerford
Tibooburra
Yantabulla
Enngonia
Marree
Milparinka
Wanaaring
Fords Bridge
Bowan River
BOURKE
Lyndhurst
Leigh Creek
Andamooka
Lake Frome
Lake Torrens
Louth
Joulnie
White Cliffs
Blinman
WOOMERA
Darling River
Wilcannia
COBAR
Yanco Glen
Mount Gipps
Bookaloo
Hawker
Nymag

Boats in the Desert

Rex Ellis

First published in 2006 by Central Queensland University Press

Second published in 2012 by Boolarong Press, Salisbury, Brisbane, Australia.

National Library of Australia Cataloguing-in-Publication entry

Author:	Ellis, Rex, 1942-
Title:	Boats in the desert / Rex Ellis.
ISBN:	9781921920646 (pbk)
Subjects:	Ellis, Rex, 1942---Travel.
	Safari guides--Australia--Biography.
	Safaris--Australia.
	Boats and boating--Australia.
	Deserts--Australia.
	Australia--Description and travel.
Dewey Number:	919.4047

Typeset by Watson Ferguson & Company

Printed and bound by Watson Ferguson and Company, Salisbury, Brisbane, Australia.

To Rainer, Solomon & Kale

FOREWORD

An invitation to write a foreword is flattering: I accepted with alacrity. It also includes the privilege of a pre-proof preview; thus, I am able to predict confidently that all comers will derive great pleasure from this, the latest distillation of Rex Ellis' campfire yarns.

As the title suggests, this volume is about small craft in (mostly) inland watercourses, rather than Rex's customary "Ships" of the Desert. The only camels encountered are those marooned by floodwaters.

These stories are factual accounts of real-life deeds. Exciting and verifiable; shorn of raconteur's licence. The characters, including the extended Ellis family of Jack Russell terriers, Trouble and Stubby, are equally real and identifiable.

Yours truly, may search these pages in vain for the obsessive "Regular" Reg, the eccentric "Two-mile" Sheedy and the breathtaking practical jokes we associate with Rex and his friends, but in their place you will experience genuine fearfulness and vividly recreated atmosphere. You will be thrilled by the adventures of those in peril on the (inland) sea. You will chuckle at the understated Ellis humour; you will identify with the Murray River angler, ambushed by the swift and silent "Magic Carpet" and with the weary wanderer, unwittingly sharing his sleeping bag with a large Western Brown!

Rex has never claimed (so far as I know) to be the Patrick White of The Tanami but he can wax lyrical at the sight of a sunset on Lake Frome, or a red sand-dune carpeted with wildflowers - and he can take you there with him.

His literary style is based on a solid foundation of oral storytelling. While reading the lines, you hear the words - as many of us have heard them by the dim and flaring lamps, sipping cask- red by the watch fires of a hundred circling camps. As the late Mr N. Lindsay pointed out to readers of The Magic Pudding, "if you don't sit by a camp fire in the evening, you have to sit by nothing in the dark, which is a most unsociable way of spending your time!"

Readers who have accompanied Rex on safari will find this book a nostalgic reminder of days - and nights - on the track. Those taking their first steps into Ellis-land will find it compulsive reading, likely to engender an irresistible urge to join Rex and Patti around the campfire.

Harry Bell.
Retired Judge and Chairman of Quarter Sessions

INTRODUCTION

Australia is probably the only country in the world where you can put a boat in a river, and follow it inland, away from the sea. That's just one reason that makes boating in the desert in Australia, a truly unique experience.

My earlier trips were part of vehicle trip base camps, where we would spend two or three days using the boats to explore various inland waters.

In 1973, the Georgina River ran a good flood again, causing Eyre Creek to run through the Eastern Simpson Desert emptying into Goyders Lagoon Swamp. This gave the opportunity for the first of our many trips where we followed flooding rivers.

These are probably my favourite outback experiences. There are numerous hazards, but once you are familiar with them, it's usually plain sailing.

Almost every camp is idyllic, with ever present birdlife. The icing on the cake is for the country to be in good heart as well, particularly in the winter, with masses of wild flowers. Not so in summer months, because the flies can be as bad as they ever are with green herbage and hot weather.

Because of the rare weather events that cause inland flooding, it is often years between trips. I watch the weather patterns, and have mates scattered around the country who ring me up if a river looks like getting water in it. I then have to contact my list of potential river runners to get a party together in a hurry. It's not a matter of missing the boat, but of missing the river. On the shorter rivers you have to catch the start of the flood and stay with it otherwise you run out of water, and either don't get a start, or get marooned in some inaccessible place.

If I can't get a party together in a short time, I'll often go anyway, with a few mates, too good to miss.

We use big heavy duty Stacer aluminium punts with canvas canopies, very comfortable seating with backrests. It's so comfortable that you often have to talk people into having a leg stretch stop between meals.

Like most of our camel treks, you rarely see another soul.

Rex Ellis.

CONTENTS

1

Coongie Lakes

The Coongie Lakes are without doubt one of the jewels of the outback. Located in the far north east of South Australia, they are fed by the north west channel of Cooper Creek and are in the northern Strzelecki Desert. The main complex of near permanent water comprises Lakes Coongie, Tidlawonnie, Marracoochannie, Marracoolcannie, and Marrandippadippa (Lake Goyder), other nearby lakes that sometimes contain water are Massacre, Apanburra, Sir Richard and Lady Blanche.

They are arguably the largest body of permanent fresh water in Central Australia. It has only been in the occasional years when the tropical monsoons have all but failed that the main lakes have not been covered in water, in particular, Coongie, Tidlawonnie, Marracoochannie and Marrcoolcannie.

Practically every year Cooper Creek runs a channel of water down to Embarka Waterhole, just north of the Moomba gas fields. At the same time some 50 kilometres west of Innamincka, the north west channel heads out pouring white water into Coongie Lakes.

If the flood is a big one, water overflows Embarka Waterhole inundating Tirra Warra Swamp and beginning one of the world's truly remarkable irregular flooding events. Water slowly covers vast cane grass and lignum swamps, rushes along narrow channels into still further swamps, waterholes and vast floodplains. This is when Cooper Creek can be over 100 miles wide.

If it is a gigantic flood (usually combining a long monsoon season coupled with exceptional inland rains) the total Coongie Lakes complex overflows, and a series of channels and flood flats carry that water west then south to join the waters from the main channel. When this occurs water will inevitably cross the Birdsville Track and run down to Lake Eyre.

I first laid eyes on Coongie Lakes in 1966, soon after getting into the safari business. It was on one of the many school trips I took for the late Charles Fisher, on the occasion when he was headmaster of Scotch College in Adelaide. I had a 12 foot flat bottomed aluminium punt that I used on the long permanent waterholes near Innamincka. We went out to Coongie on a little "wheel track" road, taking a couple of hours to travel the 100kms. We were intending to set up a four day base camp at Coongie Lakes to thoroughly explore the area. The then manager of Innamincka, Kenny Kemp had okayed this trip and his younger brother (Snowy) gave me a lot of valuable information when I passed through Kudrimitchie Outstation, located on Kudrimitchie Waterhole, some 18kms from Coongie.

In those days, and up to around the late 1970's, it was very rare to see a tourist vehicle at Coongie. Each year I would visit Coongie at least a couple of times, staying for varying periods, and it wasn't until the four wheel drive boom in the mid seventies, that we no longer had it to ourselves. It was at that time I decided to begin using camels in the business. When (especially during the school holidays) the traffic really began to build up, I would re-route my 4WD safaris, coming directly from Birdsville cross country over the desert to the west side of the lakes, giving us complete privacy, which is what I tried to guarantee my parties.

Anyway, getting back to the 1966 trip – we planned an overnight boat trip over to Lake Tidlawonnie, which is also sometimes known as Toontawaronnie, supposedly an Aboriginal name meaning "stinking feet".

Charles Fisher, two lads and myself set off one morning, towing a small rubber inflatable with extra fuel and non-perishables. Our base camp was one of those marvellous bush camps, located on a low firm sand dune that was the high bank of the north west channel. We were shaded by picturesque River Red Gums, the narrow channel making a marvellous swimming hole, with the other bank belonging to a long island that ran almost down to the lake. About 150m in front of us the sand dune gently fell away to Lake Coongie in all its beauty. Like most of the lakes it is ringed by mostly red sand dunes. Between the lake beach and the small dunes there is a thick stand of coolibah, old and gnarled, excellent shade and excellent firewood.

We launched the boat in the channel idling the Mercury outboard along a narrow channel overhung by gums and river coobah (Acacia Stenaphylla). I had four vehicles on this trip and my other drivers were looking after the main group of kids until we returned.

The birdlife between our camp (near the ruins of the old Coognie homestead, just a few standing posts and some corrugated iron) and the open lake, is amongst some of the most interesting in outback Australia, and a delight for ornithologist and layman alike. You simply cannot ignore it, a flock of pink eared duck, cormorants and various water hens fly past within arms reach each side of the narrow channel. Overhead can be several, or hundreds of black and whistling kites, while the gums are alive with little corellas and galahs, making conversation impossible. Kingfishers dart by, while the low shrubs and undergrowth are alive with wrens, zebra finch and other small birds. A veritable ornithological feast. Unfortunately since the invasion of tourists, the birdlife in this concentrated area has diminished alarmingly. The topography is such that tourists are funnelled into the beautiful cul-de-sac between the channel and the lake. It is now a conservation park and National Parks have endeavoured to restrict and control the masses, but things will never be the same.

After a while we passed the end of the island and travelled through a classic estuary – low sandy spits only metres wide covered in low reeds and sedges. It extended some hundred odd metres into the lake, its end marked by the flock of pelicans and various waders including the exquisite red necked avocet.

It was a good feeling to enter the open lake, which was probably around six or seven square kilometres in area. We could see our camp getting smaller and smaller as I made for the north eastern side. We were vulnerable to wind in our heavily laden boat, and I was keen to be in close proximity to the shore. Coongie Lake has a beautiful shoreline. A short sandy beach averaging about eight metres before you reach the beautiful old coolibahs. Our shadiest eucalypt is also a great accommodation provider for our wildlife. Similar to red gums, the older trees are full of hollows. Consequently after good rains they swarm with budgerigars, cockatiels (the world's smallest cockatoo), galahs, corellas and other hollow nesting birds.

The underside of the main branches is often covered with clusters of bottle shaped mud nests belonging to fairy martins, while the closely related tree martins use the smaller hollows. It's a sight to see a fairy martin enter their nest through a hole barely bigger than themselves, without reducing speed.

Bats, goannas and other reptile fauna also use the hollows, not to mention countless insect species. The dead and live branches harbour the nests of spoonbills, herons, egrets and thousands of cormorants and darters. Some coolibahs put you in mind of an overcrowded apartment block in some third world country, and you wonder that the health of the tree is not affected. In addition, coolibah is one of the finest cooking timbers, along with myall and gidgea, in the world. Fence posts cut from coolibah stand in the ground for well over 100 years. acacia micro theca (meaning "small seed") would have my vote as one of Australia's most interesting and useful trees. Even cattle eat the leaves in dry times.

Behind the coolibahs is usually to be found a red sand dune, its sand running down past the trunks of the rear coolibahs and coobahs. In the good years you get a few large annuals growing down the slopes and around the coolibahs, but mostly the ground is bare of undergrowth. The tops of the dunes carry the usual perennials such as sturt pea (Crotalaria), sand hill cane grass, white wood (Attalaya) and in the years of good rain they are covered with the great show of everlastings and other flowering plants. I can't think of any better desert floor show than around Coongie Lakes in a good year. The country is a splash of riotous colour, and the air full of the music of song larks and other songsters of the bird world.

In a drought year they are probably the best example of an outback "oasis" you would find, particularly when the rabbits have eaten out the surrounding dune country. You travel through a desolate wasteland of drifting sand and straccy trees and the dry sticks of dead undergrowth. Coming to the top of a sand hill you are suddenly confronted with a lake of often blue water (depending on the time of day) surrounded by its ring of grey green coolibahs – a sight to gladden the heart.

It is interesting that when Burke and Wills travelled through here in 1860, no mention was made of these lakes, except Lake Massacre where Charlie Gray was buried on their way back from the gulf. That was dry as it mostly is, but the whole lake complex must have been dry not to rate a mention

After landing for a leak, we motored along the shoreline until we came to the channel that leads from Coongie into Tidlawonnie. Actually the short channel first runs into another smaller open expanse of water, that Snowy Kemp refers to as Lake Milkamillanie, although I have never seen this on any maps old or new - it is just shown as part of Lake Coongie.

We landed here and walking around came across more Aboriginal stone artefacts than I have ever seen in one location. This goes for the Coongie Lakes region in general. Practically all of this material has been carried in, as there is no natural stone in the area until you reach the Gibber Plains of Sturt Stony Desert. Some of the bottom grinding stones were so big (up to a metre long) that it was a job to lift them. It is interesting to speculate when they were first carried in and from where. You find definite campsites with the grinding faces of the stones turned down, presumably to protect them from the elements – I have never heard any other reason for this.

We found greenstone axes that I later found out were traded from Gippsland in Victoria. The wooden handles were usually fixed to these with kangaroo sinew, but were long rotted away. Some axes were as small as tobacco tins, while I have since found others on the Georgina River as large as small dinner plates. The camps are usually littered with scrapers, known as "tules" or when worn away as to be of no further use, they are called 'tule slugs". Beautifully carved "pirri points" with their serrated edges are sometimes found (often traded). The more recent are made from glass bottles, a source of material that must have delighted the Aboriginal craftsmen. There were top grinding stones, often sitting on or near the bottom of the "bottom grinders". Most of these were roundish with a smooth bottom face, but sometimes you would find large bottom grinding stones with a narrow long grinding face. The top grinder for this is cylindrical, and the seed etc ground with a long rubbing motion as distinct from the rounder stones. Horses for courses. These stones are usually referred to as "nardoo stones". The Nardoo seed (actually a type of fern) grows in great profusion on the flood flats after and as the water recedes. Whole plants sometimes as far as the eye can see, will be covered in an attractive burnished copper colour. The actual seeds are small and brown and these were a great staple in the diet of Aboriginal people in flood country. The Aboriginal women would make their "nardoo cakes", a not too nutritious food but important nevertheless.

We spent an hour or so collecting a third of a pannikin of seeds and then crushed them with a couple of "nardoo stones", a long tedious process. With a little bit of water we "constructed" a shapeless mass we called a cake, and collectively ate it. It was only half a mouthful for a small boy, but we all had a taste and pronounced it "terrible"! No taste.

I have since spent half a day with Linda Crombe one of the Birdsville Aboriginal women, collecting seeds and making a cake. She was an expert, but despite her experience and dedication, Balfours never need have fear of a Cooper Creek competitor!

That night we made camp on the north side of Lake Tidlawonnie, a delightful spot in a small inlet of relatively deep water surrounded by old coolibahs. Everything you could possibly need including good wood, shade, water, hard sand and even aesthetics.

The lads were keen to fish and I told them all they were likely to catch out in the lakes were bony bream, which are impossible to eat. They have more bones than your average cemetery. They caught a dozen and chucked them back in. It's a bit different in the channels and waterholes where the yellow belly and black bream comprise probably the best fresh water fish eating in the world, absolutely delectable.

Next morning we had a look at a few Aboriginal graves located along the tops of the sand hills overlooking the lake, they are buried about a metre or so deep. Coolibah logs are then laid longitudinally along the grave, mostly around two metres long and presumably to stop dingoes digging up the remains. It is interesting to observe that the logs on some of the newer graves (since the coming of Europeans) have been cut with a steel axe, evidence by the clean cuts on the end of the logs. There is a very good example of this on a large grave near Mulkembah Waterhole, on the Cooper, near Innamincka.

We loaded up and headed out into Marroocutchanie Lakes, spending a bit of time walking around on the other side before boiling the billy for lunch. I shot three black ducks to contribute to the evening meal, before starting off for our base camp. This time we followed the opposite shoreline around, back up through the pristine beauty of the estuary and around the opposite side of the island where the channel is wider. It was literally black with waterfowl, including thousands of coots, to top it off, a black breasted buzzard (one of the most beautiful and interesting raptors) was making low passes over large black tail native hens. We could see the campfire through the bush, and arrived back just after sundown, a very worthwhile little trip. I didn't realise it then, but it was to be the first of many desert boat safaris that I would operate.

A couple of year's later, using three boats; I operated a three day trip getting right out to Lake Marrandippadippa.

2

The Lake Eyre Crossing

I was looking after the Birdsville Pub in January 1974 when the idea slowly crystallised. As the month progressed there were reports almost daily of huge downpours of rain in the inland – up to 250mm in 24 hours on the Birdsville Track! The days were warm and muggy with the temperature barely making the mid -30's unlike the usual January temperatures of between 38 to 40 degrees.

There had been a good monsoon in North Queensland, and the consequence of all this was that the major inland rivers were all racing in full flood towards the dry bed of Lake Eyre. The Diamantina was up to 50 kilometres wide in places and had cut Birdsville off. I had a Range Rover stranded on an island in the river not far from the pub – in fact I could see it from the bar.

For a long while I had wondered what it would be like to cross Lake Eyre by boat, never really expecting to get the opportunity. But now I felt very sure that Lake Eyre must fill, with the Cooper, Diamantina, and Georgina Rivers registering record floods. So I made my plans.

In March 1974, five of us drove north in one of my four wheel drive International wagons. There was Vincent Serventy, the well known naturalist, Jim Dorward, a storekeeper from Hawker, Frank Jack, a journalist, Gerald Day, an earthmoving contractor from Clare and myself.

We travelled up the deserted Birdsville Track to the highway department's ferry on Cooper Creek. Speed was the essence because the ferry or punt was about to be marooned by rising water, probably within a day or so, according to Brian Oldfield at Etadunna Station, whose country much of the Cooper runs through. On top of the truck were a 3.5 metre aluminium flat-bottomed punt, and another one inside the back, about a metre protruding. We carried sufficient fuel and stores for nine days' boat travel, plus necessary gear.

When we arrived at the ferry landing we could see that it was on the far bank, about 100 metres distant with no-one in attendance. After a short discussion on the pros and cons of waiting, Gerry and I decided we would swim across and bring it back to our side. We walked upstream about 200 metres and entered the fast-flowing water. The swim took us about 10 minutes, and the current carried us 100 metres downstream from the punt. We weren't sorry to crawl out the other side. We walked up to the punt, started the two small outboard motors, and brought it back to the south bank.

It didn't take us long to load the truck and start across. As we did a Toyota pulled up on the north bank, and Devin Daw from Mulka Station jumped out. He had his kids with him to do a bit of fishing. We unloaded, had a yarn to Kevin and went on our way.

Late that afternoon we arrived at Cowarie Station owned by Claude Oldfield. The main track to Kalamurina Station was under water and cut off, so Oldfield gave us directions for getting there over the sand hills. We jumped several 24 metre hills with the truck's Sahara sand tyres well down, but the dark and some very steep 30 metre hills stopped us. Thinking that we had done enough for one day we made camp.

The next morning we followed the big sand hill down until it ran into floodwater. We decided that we would launch the boats here giving Gerry more time to get back over the Cooper before access to the ferry was cut off. It took us nearly an hour to unload the boats and pack the assorted gear in. We carried 270 litres of two stroke fuel in 12 jerry cans. Other fluid consisted of six flagons of red and white wine and several cartons of canned beer. We had fresh meat that would last three days, some salt beef, packet spaghetti and rice. Tins were kept to a minimum, but we did have daily rations of fruit juice, canned milk, canned fruit and rice cream. There was rye bread for nearly a week and self-raising flour for dampers. Margarine, sugar, tea, coffee, boiled fruit cake and fresh fruit and vegetables were among the rest of the stores.

The boats were equipped with an outboard motor each. One had a seven horse power Mercury and the other punt, which would be towed, had a little one and half horse power Seagull as an auxiliary motor. Our gear included a radio transceiver and car battery, a combination shotgun-rifle for shooting rabbits and ducks when we ran out of meat, fishing gear, cooking gear and utensils, life jackets, cameras binoculars, film, swags and personal baggage. Each of the two punts had three metre bows over which a canvas sheet was stretched. This was to keep the sun off, as it was still the tail end of summer. We half unrolled the swags on the bottom of the boat so that each person could recline with a considerable degree of comfort. The beer was placed under the swags on the bottom of the boat – almost a natural fridge.

We pushed off at about 10.30am leaving Gerry looking as if he was being marooned on a desert island. We arranged to meet him in approximately six days time at Level Post Bay on the southern end of Lake Eyre North.

The water was only about 30cms deep for the first one and half kilometres, but as we neared the main channel it deepened, and a current could be detected. Both boats were heavily laden, but still had about 15cm free board. Frank chose to ride alone in the rear boat, rolling his swag out on top of the fuel and wine.

After a few kilometres we found the inlet that led to Kalumurina Station, the home of Jim and Joan Dunn. The unprecedented flood had been right through their relatively high homestead, which had been built approximately six metres above the previous record flood level. When Gerry and I had recently landed at Kalumurina on an aerial recce of the river and lake, Jim had told us how a great wall of water had finally broken his levee bank and enveloped the house. Joan had recorded this on an 8mm movie camera, even though she couldn't see for the tears.

We pulled into the base of the sand hill and started to unload some fresh vegetables for Jim. Jim Dunn and two of his men met us, and after unloading the stores, invited us up for lunch. He noted it was somewhat unusual to have their stores brought by river. Jim and the boys put on a magnificent three course lunch for us in their well-equipped camp on top of the sand hill. He told us they had killed a great number of snakes in and around the hut and camp. Flooding usually means an increase in snakes, and there were also many native rats in the country.

Jim was interested in our proposed journey, and gave us some valuable information about the river. He and Claude Oldfield had lost considerable numbers of cattle in the flood, and Jim said that he had several mobs stranded on islands downstream. We agreed to keep our eyes open for these and to pull some scrub for them where possible. Jim had recently purchased a boat and had been carting some baled hay to some of the islands where cattle were stranded. He hoped to keep them alive until such time as the river dropped and they were able to walk out under their own steam.

He was particularly interested in how we were going to fare crossing Lake Eyre, and we told him we had rubber dinghies we were going to blow up and tie alongside for sleeping purposes. When he asked about toilet facilities I was at a bit of a quandary because I hadn't really considered those, so as a parting gesture, he presented us with a wooden toilet seat that had come down with the floods. He jokingly suggested that we could perhaps tie this between the two boats, and that it would make an admirable toilet. We all agreed that it was an excellent idea and in the meantime, that it would serve as quite a comfortable back rest in the boats.

It was about 3.30p.m. when we left Kalumurina and headed off downstream. Soon we passed some very large sand hills where the ends had been completely cut off, as with a knife, by initial floodwater. Right from the beginning the bird life had been plentiful and varied. There were half a dozen species of duck present along with the larger water birds such as white-faced and pacific herons, yellow-billed spoonbills, great egrets and cormorants. On one occasion we came across the carcass of a cow caught high in the branches of a coolabah tree by its horns. It was difficult to know how far down the river this beast had been washed and no doubt there were many more in the same predicament.

We camped that evening on the northern bank of the river on a small flat backed by the huge sand hill, an idyllic camp with budgerigars everywhere. We had a hearty meal consisting of soup, steak and onions, tinned fruit and rice cream washed down with several glasses of red wine. We were in great spirits and keenly anticipating the journey ahead. Boats had never before been down the Cooper, and there were many unknown quantities, but this made it all the more interesting.

I talked that evening to a friend on a radio transceiver and gave our location. We did this most evenings, the radio being our one and only contact with civilisation. The battery that we carried was fully charged and with limited use it would see out the duration of the trip.

That evening in our swags we heard the lowing of cattle, and on quite a few occasions, dingoes calling. We reckoned this would be where Jim Dunn's cattle were stranded, and it proved to be the case next morning when we sailed several kilometres across to an island on the south side of the river. Here were some 80 head of cattle many of them in poor condition, and several carcasses scattered around. Although we didn't see any dingoes, we saw fresh tracks, and it was obvious that there were several dingoes stranded with the cattle, and very much enjoying the enforced stay. We telegrammed Jim Dunn by radio notifying him of the situation. After pulling some scrub for the cattle, we pushed off down the river, cutting off towards the main channel. This was probably one of the most idyllic days that we experienced, lying back in the boats and just following a fairly well-defined channel. We did have a little excitement on one occasion when we were suddenly forced to negotiate a tangled mass of coolabah and river cooba trees. The water was extremely fast here, and we were very fortunate to get through this without a mishap. Our main problem was the boat following, and we didn't have time to shorten the rope. We were continually ducking our heads and breaking off smaller branches as the water thrust us through the timber. On one occasion Frank was left up in the branches of a coolabah with the back boat caught up between a low branch and the trunk. After perhaps 100 metres of this we emerged into open water and counted our lucky stars. The only damage that we suffered was a dent in the bow holding up the canvas canopy, which could be straightened out. Every now and then the motor would hit a log, but was designed to ride over these, and was no problem.

Around lunch time we headed across to the northern bank which was one and half kilometres wide at this stage, and made camp for lunch. There was quite a good beach here and we all had a swim before boiling the billy.

After lunch Vin and I spent an hour searching the surrounding sand hills for the eyrean grass wren, a rare species, but still thought to be in the area. We were not successful, but did see variegated fairy-wrens, masked wood swallows, species of quail, and a pallid cuckoo. Land birds were not as abundant as water birds, but whenever we stopped we saw something of interest, and we never really knew what we would find. Our one great hope of course, was to find the night parrot, a species presumed by many to be extinct, which possibly still does survive in some of these remote and rarely frequented areas. We did find a few Aboriginal scrapers, but no sign of any substantial campsites.

After lunch we sailed back until we hit the main channel, and soon after this Vin thought that he saw a brahminy kite (red-backed sea eagle) in the distance. It would be unusual to see this bird here, but quite possible if it had followed the flooded river down for many hundreds of kilometres. Many coastal species found themselves inland in this exceptional year.

Several times that afternoon we saw bearded dragons swimming in the water and where we could we picked them up and placed them in trees. On one occasion we found a goanna swimming across the river, but we let him continue on his way.

Later that afternoon we came across a narrow island about one and a half kilometres offshore and decided to camp here for the night. We had a ready-made harbour for the boats and pulled them in, making them fast to one of the large coolabahs on the island. This island was really the top half of a long sand hill that provided us with probably the best campsite of the whole trip. We ate the last of our fresh meat on this night, and as the sun set, lay back against our swags watching this mighty river pass on its way to the lake. It was a truly beautiful setting, and we were in no hurry for darkness to come, as the sunset was really spectacular. Most evenings Frank was busy taking notes for various articles he intended writing, while Vin prowled around seeing what else our campsite could offer us. Jim Dorward, who said he never drank red wine, found out that he did after all have a liking for the stuff, and was good company for me while I prepared the evening meal.

We were away about 7.30a.m. next morning, and conditions were mild and still. After several kilometres travel we rounded a bend to be confronted by a long line of cliffs. These cliffs were composed of many different layers in which gypsum seemed predominant, and as we came nearer, we were aware of really impressive reflections in the water. Surprisingly enough, it is possible to have tree and land forms reflected in this murky water, and everyone present exposed quite a bit of film during the next kilometre or so. As we sailed quite close into the shore under the shadow of the cliffs we noticed bits and pieces falling away, a result of the engine noise. On one occasion one quite large section of cliff fell away and we all wondered how we would have fared had we been just a few metres closer in.

Rabbits were quite common here and the bird life was interesting around the cliffs also. Crows were present all along them eyeing us in their cynical fashion, while little corellas and galahs were nesting in holes about a metre below the top of the cliff. The odd white-faced and pacific heron seemed to find food at the base of these cliffs, and we disturbed quite of few of these.

About midday we came across a small land-locked harbour surrounded by cliffs and pulled in for lunch. There were quite tall coolabahs here, and it was a pleasant spot. Nearby, sand hills spilled down over the cliff, and we spent half an hour walking up to the top, over and away from the river. To the south of us the sand hills shimmered in the midday heat and despite the good cover of herbage, their sterility was very apparent. To the north, east and west, however, it was a different world altogether from our position on this sand hill. It was a combination of cliffs, islands, water and trees, and far in the distance the high sand hills on the other side of the river. From positions like this it was no trouble to see the path of the river, and we often had to do this in order to check the correct channel.

We spent a good hour on top of this sand hill, feeling no incentive to move. This was the pattern of the last few days, and I am sure that is where the real therapy lies in this type of outback travel. To move and do things only when one wants to is getting to be a rare thing in this day and age. Our only real commitment was a rendezvous with Gerry in about six days' time, and I think everybody was only just beginning to appreciate this. Frank and Jim had left busy occupations or businesses behind them, although Vin maintained that he was "on the job" right now. Myself also, except that this was quite a way removed from my usual trip where I have deadlines to meet. We reluctantly left our hill and descended to our shaded anchorage for lunch.

Not long after leaving our lunch camp we again pulled into an interesting-looking spot in the cliffs. While I was walking across what looked like dry watercourse, the top crust broke and I plunged to my waist in thick glutinous mud, a type of quicksand, and although I probably would have extricated myself in time, I was very glad of the others' assistance. After much laughter and several photographs, they dragged me out of the mud trap and I retreated to the river for a clean-up. We examined some huge gypsum crystals, the biggest I had ever seen. Many were 25 to 30cms across with light-coloured zigzag lines running through them. One always felt somewhat temporary around the base of these cliffs, and never really knowing when several tonnes were going to break off and fall into the river.

After a few more kilometres we left the cliffs behind us, finding ourselves out in the middle of a very large body of water. It was here that Jim drew our attention to a mysterious spectacle in the water ahead of us. From about 30 metres it appeared to be a piece of rope or something similar projecting some way out of the water and going round and around in the current. As we drew close we could see that it was the tail of a very large brown snake sticking straight up out of the water. We speculated that it must have been diving to escape the boats, for we could see no other reason for such an unusual manoeuvre, unless it was pursuing something underwater, but this seemed unlikely. As we both drifted together in the current we made several circles around the snake, photographing its unusual behaviour, and on our third run the snake came up for air. From the time we had first seen it, it had been underwater for at least three minutes. It was probably a king brown snake, nearly two metres long, and not at all happy with our presence. If we came too close it would swim towards the boat with the obvious intention of boarding it. After several more close-up photographs we continued on our way, having no desire to take on such a passenger.

We were getting well down the river now, and we had to keep our eyes open for a channel that turned off to the south, ending in a cul-de-sac about 65 kilometres from the river. This was known as Karawarina Creek. If we got into this without knowing it, it could give us no end of trouble. The trip back against the current would not be as much fun, as we could only make one and half kilometres an hour in that direction. We avoided this channel, but ran out of deep water in several other backwaters that we entered by mistake. In one place we were forced to push the boats 100 metres or so before getting back into a sufficient depth of water. There were sandbars in the main channel also, and the secret was to find the channels that led through them. We did this by testing the depth with an oar as we travelled, but very often the strong current would sweep us out of the channels into the shallower water, and we were forced to make our slow way back to them.

About 5p.m. we broke into a very large body of water two kilometres across, with a complete absence of timber on both shores, I remembered this from our aerial survey, and estimated we were only about three kilometres from the lake.

A little while later we came to another channel, and I couldn't for the life of me make up my mind which was the correct one. It was here that a strange thing happened. There was storm activity in the region, with quite a lot of cloud in the western sky. Sitting just above one of these channels was a piece of cloud shaped in the form of a broad arrow and pointing down on one particular channel. We all agreed whether we were Christian or atheist, that we could not possibly ignore a sign like this. Mentally thanking whoever was responsible, we headed confidently into this channel, making camp several kilometres further on, on a timberless shore. Just before dark I walked to the top of the highest rise and came to the conclusion that we were not where we were supposed to be. We gathered sufficient wood for a small cooking fire and bedded down for the night. It wasn't one of the most memorable camps.

After breakfast next morning we emptied the front boat of most of the gear and on my own, I took off on a reconnaissance. I could travel three times our normal speed, and with the nose of the punt high in the air, I confirmed the fact that it was an island, and that there were no more channels down this end. As we were flying low during our aerial survey, and I was on the right-hand side of the plane, I must have completely missed this small backwater and island. I returned to our camp, loaded up once again, and we were on our way. We soon reached the main body of water again and on following the shore around, came to a small island.

On the horizon we could see two brumbies. There was a black stallion and mare, and they followed our progress for about a kilometre. Then we observed nine camels, also on the horizon, and walking along the top of the sand hill. It was too much for us, and we headed the boats into shore hoping to get some photographs. I had a

16mm movie camera; Vin had his big camera and telephoto lens, while Frank and Jim had 35mm cameras.

We walked up the sand hill towards the camels that by this time had stopped and were eyeing us intently. As we neared them we began filming and when we were some 300 metres distance they had all turned and ran back towards the other end of the island. When we reached the top of the sand hill we observed that the island was about 120 hectares in area and noticed that it was only an island because of the exceptionally high flood. A narrow neck of land that was normally joined to the mainland was slowly appearing, but this was obviously too boggy yet to allow the horses and camels to escape their confinement. There was still plenty of feed around for them, but the interesting thing to us was that both horses and camels were running together in what appeared to be perfect harmony. Here were two traditional rivals forced by their mutual predicament to make the best of each other's company. We moved down towards them and took a good close-up film of the horses running shoulder to shoulder with the camels. This was, we thought, some very worthwhile film and I was particularly pleased to obtain a movie of this unusual occurrence. The animals were in good condition, and it was evident that they would make it off the island when the crossing permitted.

After another kilometre or so we saw the mouth of the Diamantina. A little further on we went between two large sand hills on either side of the mouth, and in front of this was nothing but water and sky. We were there at last.

It was an exciting moment for us all as we sailed down towards the mouth of the Diamantina knowing that we were the first boat party ever to come down this river from the Birdsville Track to Lake Eyre. It had taken us exactly three days to make the voyage, and it was about 10a.m. when we arrived. We returned to the southern side of the mouth and made camp. We walked up this sand hill and looked out across the muddy inland sea. All we could see was the most sterile and desolate part of Australia at its all-time best; instead of the white glare of salt, sand hills and parched watercourse there was a vast lake with white caps breaking its surface. There were gently rolling hills covered in green herbage and wildflowers and through the mouth came life-giving fresh water at the rate of hundreds of millions of litres per hour.

We spent all day here, and it was strange to observe that, depending on the amount of cloud around or the time of day, the lake surface varied quite considerably in colour from green through blue, to a brown the same colour as the river running through the mouth.

We took the boat across to the other side of the mouth and explored some interesting hard sand country where the water and wind had eroded huge miniature canyons up to 10 metres deep, which in some places were like a maze. On the bottom were the tracks of snakes, dingoes, rabbits, and other small animals and birds. It did enter my mind that it could be interesting to encounter a dingo under the circumstances. In some places it would be very difficult to turn around and impossible to climb up the sides, and so the meeting could produce a very interesting experiment in dingo-human relationships.

Most of the day we spent sorting out gear, swimming, and generally exploring the areas. On one occasion while Vin and I were in the water swimming, one of the native long-haired rats went past us in the current, and out in the waters of the lake. We tried to rescue it, but it attacked us quite fiercely, so we let it go. Thousands of animals and reptiles must be washed down in this fashion and later on we were to find the bodies of many of them.

All day long the lake waters had been quite rough with a fairly stiff breeze blowing, and when we did try the waters of the lake in our boats the waves were high enough to give us some cause for alarm. The more we thought about this the more they would see problems ahead in our intentions of crossing Lake Eyre from the north to south. Soon after the sun had sunk into the lake that evening, I suggested to the party that we make the crossing at night. For a moment I think they questioned my sanity, but after we discussed it they realised that there wasn't a great deal of difference from making the crossing during daylight hours. It was my contention that the wind would be far less at night, and at night we had the Southern Cross for navigation. Even in the day-time all we would be able to see would be the water and sky, so in this regard there wasn't a great deal of difference. Everyone was quite happy about the crossing, and all of our valuable equipment had been insured in case of mishap. We wore life belts at all times in the boats and our flat-bottomed aluminium craft were unsinkable.

And so it was that after considerable discussion on the matter, we set off from our camp on the mouth, heading in a south-westerly direction on to the lake. I think we all felt very insignificant as our tiny crafts made their way across the mirror-like surface. The water reflected the last light of the day and the scene was one of peace and tranquillity. At this stage we had less than a metre of water, and we were trying to find the Warburton Groove to get out into deeper water. The Groove, which is the channel cut by the Diamantina when it runs its normal floodwaters into the lake, can easily be seen from the air, and it was apparent to us in March when we flew down the lake – in fact we followed it down to Brooks Island. The channel varies from about 20 to 60 metres wide, and after the river stops' running it becomes a narrow strip of brine running almost three quarters of the length of the lake. We had not been able to find it from the sand hills around the mouth, and could not find it now by depthing it with one of the oars. We probably went over the top of it without realising it, as it may have been quite shallow at this point.

After an hour or so of searching we gave it away and went on a south-westerly course. At 8p.m. we stopped the boats, having travelled some 13kms out from shore. With some effort we erected the 11 metre telescopic transceiver aerial in the boat and made radio contact with Adelaide. After a brief talk we dismantled the aerial and continued on our way. It was now pitch dark. We were progressing well, and we all began making ourselves comfortable for the long night ahead. Suddenly, we felt a light breeze on our faces, becoming stronger and stronger, until after about two minutes we had a howling wind and waves 50cms high. The suddenness of the change stunned us and we realised we were in a very tricky position.

Our anchor consisted of one and half metre star droppers (steel posts) which could be bolted together with a steel loop welded on one end. Frank jumped over the side and held this while we drove it into the bottom of the lake. The water here was about a metre deep, and Frank got thoroughly drenched, not expecting the knee-deep mud that went with it. Unfortunately the bolts were not high tensile, and after the second blow with the sledge hammer, they sheared off in the holes, It left us with only one post, so we drove this in until it disappeared under the surface of the water, and Frank pulled himself back into the rear boat. It appeared that we were still moving, not being held by the somewhat reduced anchor. It was pitch dark and there was such turbulence in the water that we had no way of knowing if we were still anchored or were drifting northwards. This was a frightening thought, because we could be blown up on the northern shore and quite easily become stranded when the wind dropped. We could be there for days, or even weeks waiting for a similar wind to bring back enough water to enable us to float both the boats off.

On both boats we had canvas tied across the bows so as to deflect waves to both sides, and on the front boat we pulled the canvas canopy right down to one side, which gave it another 30cms of freeboard. The front boat had an octopus strap tied across the bow, and from this we draped a large sheet of polythene through the front of the boat and about two metres under the boat. This proved to be a very good wave deflector also, and I think it saved us from being swamped that night.

After attending to these matters we had no option but to stick it out, bailing all the time with various receptacles. In retrospect I realise it was the loneliest night of my life, as it was, too, for Frank, alone in the rear boat.

As the waves raced past it was impossible to tell whether we were moving or stationary. We actually had the impression of moving at a great pace through the water into the waves, but this was only an illusion. I wasn't game to go to the front of the boat to check the steel post in case we dislodged it. The waves were so large now, up to a metre high, that to move the front would increase the risk of swamping. None of us were really cold because we were bailing continuously. By about midnight we realised we would probably be safe provided the waves became no higher. Sometimes an extra large wave would hit the boat and we would bail frantically for some minutes, always managing to clear the water.

In the early hours we resurrected the old transistor radio we had, and picked up most stations across Australia. Particularly interesting to us was Father Bob's programme from Adelaide. We listened patiently as he gave counsel to all sorts of people in all sorts of predicaments. Compared with ours, we reckoned most of them were pretty minor. I would dearly have loved to give him a call.

In the blackness of this lake it was easy to imagine oneself in the middle of the Atlantic or Pacific, and it was no consolation that we only had one metre of water under us. We would doze, only to be woken up by the arrival of a larger wave, causing us to bail once more. We did have breaks in the bailing, but they were few and far between and they didn't last very long. Periodically I would yell out to Frank to see if he was still awake, fearing that he would be swamped if he went to sleep back there. Frank went to sleep quite often having only himself for company. It was far easier for the three of us, being together.

I had long since given up looking at my watch, and after what seemed an eternity, the morning star slowly rose above the horizon in the east. Daylight had never been more welcome, and very soon the sky began to lighten and we could finally see around us. What we observed didn't make us jump up and down with glee. Our only lift was that our miserable anchor had actually held us throughout the night and we had not drifted, as we had feared. Just as the sun appeared out of the water, the wind veered round to the south-west, so we decided to try and make a break for the coast. We managed to pull the anchor up, as we turned broadside on to the waves, we very nearly swamped both boats.

We set a course running half with the waves and half cutting across them, travelling roughly north-east. Despite a certain degree of worry, it was quite an interesting trip into shore some 20kms distant. We seemed to be careering along at a terrific pace with the engine alternating between full, half and idling. As a wave reared up off the corner of the rear boat I would apply my throttle accordingly. Sometimes we were almost immobile in the trough of a wave, and it seemed impossible that the wave hanging over us would not fill the boats and swamp us. This did not happen, however.

About 9a.m. we sighted land and surfed into a featureless coast around 10a.m. It was the most miserable spot one could imagine, a low level coastline with a small sand dune almost a kilometre distant, but it was the most welcome piece of Mother Earth that any of us had ever experienced.

We had a meal and travelled about eight kilometres down the coast where it wasn't quite so rough. This soon became impractical, however, and at 1p.m. we landed once more. It was our intention to sleep that afternoon and to wait for the wind to drop before continuing.

We rolled our swags out on the beach about 10 metres from the water. The sun was hot, and there was no shade, but I'm sure everyone was asleep within five minutes.

The next thing I can remember is the word "snake" being shouted and as I popped myself groggily up on one elbow, I observed an interesting performance. Jimmy Dorward is a big man, and it would normally have taken him several minutes to extricate himself from his swag. In this instance though, he slid out of it like a banana losing its peel. He began rummaging among his swag looking for something, and as he did so, I saw a brown snake slithering away from Jim's swag as fast as it could go.

As I crawled out of my swag I asked Jim what he was looking for, and he replied, "My camera – if I don't get a photo of that bloody snake near my swag, my missus will never believe me!" With this he picked up his camera and headed the snake off from the sanctuary of a clump of nitre bush, and back towards his swag – then he took his photographic proof.

By this time Vin and Frank were awake and taking an active interest in the proceedings. Vin kept trying to pin the snake down with an oar so as to get a head scale count for positive identification, but I was all for letting it go, feeling we had been spared a nasty fate. The snake was now determined to get back into Jim's untidy looking swag, so we had to kill it. It was easy to see what had happened. While we were all sleeping the snake had come up to Vin's swag. Its track passed within an arm's length of Vin's, Frank's and my swags which were all relatively tidy. Jim's swag resembled a rubbish dump and the snake couldn't believe its good luck. It went in behind a piece of mosquito netting that Jim had jammed behind his head to keep the flies away, and then must have coiled itself between his back and the swag. Jim said that a few "bugs" had been troubling him, and when he felt the movement he tried to get up on this elbow to scratch his back. The movement galvanised the snake into action, and it shot out like a Bondi tram the same way it had come in. This was when fear took over, and Jim quit his swag without having much to do with it himself!

What amazed us though was the fact that Jim showed no symptoms of shock – his biggest concern was to photograph the event to prove to his wife it had happened. When the excitement had died down we all soberly reflected on Jim's lucky escape. If he had been bitten around the head or neck, it would have meant almost certain death. I was insured for a helicopter evacuation if an emergency cropped up, but it could have been 24 hours before the patient had treatment. The common brown snake's venom is among the most deadly in the world.

I might just point out here that it is most unusual to get a snake in one's swag, but in our particular circumstances, it wasn't all that surprising. There were abnormally large populations of snakes in the country owing to the floods and the population explosion of the long-haired native rat. The snake entered Jim's swag at the time of the day when they are most active – that is, after the heat of the day has passed. The final factor was that Jim's swag and "environs" proved just too tempting in an area with very little ground cover. Most people don't roll a swag out and go to sleep in mid-afternoon.

Anyway, we all decided the place held no more attraction for us, and we moved down the coast walking along pulling the boats as the water was still too rough. We found a pleasant campsite on a small claypan backed by broken sand hill country. It was about 4.30p.m. and we rolled our swags out again and continued our interrupted slumber.

I woke up at 8.30p.m. as the sun was setting into a dead calm lake. There wasn't a breath of wind, and the sunset was one of extraordinary beauty, covering the lake with a mantle of pink and mauve. The sky was a mixture of scarlet and gold right back to the other horizon. We all sat on our swags with a can of beer taking in this display of nature until it faded to more sombre colours, and night fell. We had a quick meal and prepared the boats for departure.

Everyone shared a feeling of uneasiness after our experience of the previous night, but we had no alternative other than to carry on.

We headed off using both motors, and with the boats still attached to each other. I estimated our speed at about 15km/h. The cloud cleared almost completely, and making use of the Southern Cross, we kept on our course for Brooks Island. We were only about 20kms down the coast from the Diamantina mouth, and our course was just a few degrees east of south. With a bit of luck we hoped to hit Brooks Island in daylight, or at least be close enough to see it.

It was soon midnight, and still our luck held with the wind. Every now and then a puff of wind would ripple the satin-like lake surface, but would just as soon die away.

About 1a.m. someone produced a bottle of rum, and it would be an understatement to say that it was well received. We talked most of the time, particularly after the rum appeared, and the only time we stopped was to refuel the little Seagull outboard on Frank's boat. Every time we did this, we refuelled Frank with another nip of rum. He only had his own company back there.

Finally Mars, the brilliant morning star appeared, and I think we all reflected that our circumstances were somewhat better than when we last saw that star. Shortly afterwards the eastern sky began to colour with the piccaninny dawn, and we still held the throttles wide open. The continual drone of the motors and the slap of water against the blunt bows of the punts gave us the feeling that we had travelled hundreds of kilometres, when in fact we had done about 80.

Just as the sun came up the Mercury ran out of fuel and we stopped to refill. We looked all around us and suddenly felt very insignificant and inconsequential. Then a lone seagull flew over, had a good look, and settled on the water about 15 metres away. That cheered us up no end.

We continued on our course, and about 6a.m. a light south-easterly breeze began blowing, raising 15cm waves on the lake, and we had to reduce our speed a little. At about 9a.m. we stopped to refuel the Seagull motor and Frank stood up on a jerry can in his boat and had a look around. With some excitement he said he could see land due east of us. It was difficult to see, just a hard line on the horizon. We reckoned we must have passed to the west of Brooks Island, and headed east for the land. It proved to be about 20kms away, and as we approached, we could see a large sand hill and 12 metre cliffs on the southern end.

The closer we approached, the more we realised that this island was not Brooks Island, which is quite flat. We landed on a little rocky beach at the foot of the cliffs on the south-west corner of this island at 11a.m. We were very glad to walk on ground again, and when we climbed to the top of the sand hill we could see Brooks Island to the south-west of us. This meant that if we had kept on our original course we would have hit Brooks Island as intended. We had actually been closer to it than we were to the other island, but because of the low land, couldn't see it. We were somewhat disappointed about this, but realising this island had never been visited by whites before, we made plans to explore it.

It was about three kilometres long by about one kilometre wide at the southern end. The sand hill, which was about 18 metres above sea level, ran from the southern end to within a kilometre of the northern end. It was covered in a similar fashion to those on the eastern shore – mostly cane grass plus native herbage and grasses owing to the good season. There were quite a few "poached egg" everlastings, and large nitre bush on the lower slopes.

The bird life also was similar to that on the shore: kestrels, orange chats, pipits, crows and silver gulls were well represented. Judging by the tracks there were plenty of long-haired native rats on the island, no doubt washed up after being carried here by one of the rivers. We saw dingo tracks, and a large brown snake. Rabbits were also common.

Around the base of the 12 metre high cliffs on the southern end we found a type of modelling clay. Unfortunately, there were too many small rock particles in it for it to be ideal.

About 1.30p.m. we had a lunch of sardine sandwiches and boiled fruit cake, and all enjoyed a swim. The water at this end of the lake was quite salty and of a blue colour, compared to the brown fresh water at the northern end of the lake. Fortunately we had filled several containers on the previous day.

We had approximately 65kms to travel down Madigan Gulf to complete our crossing to Level Post Bay, and set out in high spirits around the end of the island.

We rounded the end of the island and headed at about three quarter throttle into the waves, now about 30cms high. We were supremely confident of handling anything the lake cared to throw at us. Jim Dorward was sitting up the front and complained of the spray being thrown up over the front of the boat. We had rigged polythene sheet over the blunt bow of the boat, with the bulk of the sheet draped under the boat. This served us well in deflecting any waves that lobbed on the front of the boat. I suggested that Jim pull the octopus strap and plastic higher up, and he did so, but by about half a metre. The next moment a larger than unusual wave lobbed squarely on our bow. Because there wasn't enough weight of polythene under the boat, about 250 litres of water just sat in the hollowed-out plastic sheet, right on our bow. This, coupled with the speed of the boat, caused our nose to spear under the water, bringing us to a sudden halt. I yelled to Jim to swap places, which he did with remarkable agility. I picked up the plastic bucket to bail, but when the water reached my thighs I couldn't see much sense in that.

The next few minutes were ones of mixed reaction. Vin, Jim and I stepped out of our submerged boat and floundered around in our life jackets. The boat suddenly "turned turtle" and all of our gear that didn't float went three metres down to the bottom of the lake. This included my radio transceiver, battery, 16mm movie camera, 35mm camera, and binoculars. Frank was frantically scooping up odd floating items and putting them in the rear boat. Despite the seriousness of our situation, laughter overcame me and I swallowed a fair amount of Lake Eyre. The cause of my mirth was in observing what people tried to save first. Serventy was flapping around like a pelican with a broken wing, desperately trying to salvage his cameras and bird books, while Jimmy Doward was pursuing floating cans of beer with a grim determination and depositing them in the rear punt. I noticed how fast our wooden toilet seat, the kind gift from Jim Dunn, was drifting towards Oodnadatta, and I realised the hopelessness of diving for the sunken equipment.

Our most difficult task was to get the water-logged swags back into Frank's boat. When we had recovered all that floated, we bailed out the first punt which was floating several centimetres below the surface, and climbed back in. It was about half an hour since we were swamped. Owing to the fact that the tools were on the bottom, it wasn't possible to pull the Mercury engine apart, so we had to rely on the little 1.1 kilowatt Seagull motor. We headed laboriously across to the shore about five kilometres away, landing at the north-east corner of Madigan Gulf.

We had about four hours of daylight left so we gathered a large pile of wood; using dead needlewood trees near by, and lit a bonfire to dry out our swags and gear. Vin was particularly concerned about his expensive Hasselblad camera, which had been under water. He managed to pull it apart and laid it out to dry. Most of our gear was insured, but probably our main regret was the invaluable film that we had all lost. Between us we had enough for a record, but all the movie film had gone.

By nightfall we had almost dried everything. I shot a couple of rabbits and we made a large stew of most of our remaining rations. With this and a couple of red wines settling in our stomachs, life took on a rosier tint.

We set off next morning an hour before daylight, travelling down the coat at about six km/h with the Seagull motor running flat out. The day dawned clear, warm and calm and we thoroughly enjoyed the dawn. We saw interesting "dog fights" between the two chief scavengers, the crows and the seagulls. The gulls seemed to win most of them.

Just after the sun had risen we saw two large birds flying at us. They were mountain ducks. One flew straight past, but the other circled around us, and landed about two metres from the boats. It looked at us for several seconds, and then took to the air again in fright, heading after its mate.

A pair of Emus came down, peering at us in their curious way, and followed us for some time. At one stage a dingo kept pace with us and at times we could approach within about nine metres of it. Brown falcons were very much in evidence, and several times when we stopped, there were large flocks of grey teal.

At about 10a.m. we heard the drone of an aircraft and Bluey Hughes' plane, from Muloorina Station, came in sight, approaching down the coast from north. At this stage I was walking along the shoreline easily keeping pace with the boats, and as Bluey buzzed us several times we waved that we were okay. He flew on south across Madigan Gulf and a quarter of an hour later I saw some black smoke go up on the southern horizon, indicating that Bluey had let Gerry know of our approach. This was a welcome sight to us, heralding the end of our somewhat dramatic voyage, and as the water was very calm, with no wind in evidence, we set a course straight across Madigan Gulf for the smoke. We didn't reckon that we had much else to lose, and felt quite sure that we could get "home" with the aid of the oars if necessary.

We had to refill the Seagull engine a number of times crossing the gulf, but soon saw the sand hills of Price Peninsula come into view out of a shimmering mirage. By the look of Gerry's smoke, he had enough tyres down there to start a branch of M.S. McLeod Ltd., and we had no difficulty in homing in. When we were in sight of the vehicle, we thought it was time to crack a can of beer and we had celebration drinks.

I think Gerry was gladder to see us than we were him, judging by his antics on the shore, and it was a very happy reunion when we beached the boats. There were several tourists there too.

Gerry had a big feed of steak and eggs ready for us, and we ate this ravenously, as we had only eaten in bits and pieces over the last 24 hours. We were all somewhat travel-stained in appearance, and as I had lost all of my clothes, I had a borrowed pair of shorts on.

After the meal we hopped back into the boats and sailed down to the Level Post at the bottom of Level Post Bay, and then into the Goyder Channel, following this link between the north and south lake until it ran into Lake Eyre South, where there was a party of Muloorina Station people to welcome us.

We had difficulty in making the last kilometre or so through the shallow water, leaving a large brown mud trail behind us, and it was a weary, but very satisfied crew that loaded the boats on to the International truck and headed off to Muloorina Station for a few celebration drinks.

3

Down the Diamantina – Birdsville to Lake Eyre

In 1980, we made a documentary using our camels – a re-enactment of the 1939 Madigan camel expedition across the Simpson Desert. It was called "The Madigan Line". It was filmed by Philip DeMontignies company, DeMontignie Productions.

Philip had an interest in outback stories, so I mentioned a trip I had wanted to do for some time – a boat expedition down the Diamantina River from Birdsville to Lake Eyre, having been down the Warburton section in 1974.

He liked the idea. I mentioned it to Vincent Serventy, the naturalist, who had travelled with me a lot over the years.

In the end there were five of us in the party, plus a film crew of two. The other two were Clifton Pugh, the artist and John Manning, a surveyor and Chief of National Mapping. He had undertaken the precise navigation on the "Madigan Line", locating most of Madigan's camps, which was no mean feat. He had an interest in old explorers blazed trees, and that was his mission on this trip.

Stony was my offsider on this trip, and we were using two new Avon inflatables with 15hp two stroke Yamaha outboards. A helicopter was chartered, one of its functions being to lift the expedition over Goyders Lagoon Swamp, a massive morass of lignum channels, totally un-navigable.

Duffy Sigston was our back-up man in my Blitz truck.

The night prior to departure we were camped on the Diamantina at Birdsville. It was 1981.

Next morning there was the usual bustle of trying to get maximum gear into limited space, one advantage with inflatables is that you displace very little water, no matter how much weight on board. Finding room is the main problem.

A few Birdsville people including David and Nell Brook were there to see us off, and we duly left about 9a.m. The Diamantina was still running and we poked along with motors about half throttle. I had Vincent, John and Cliff with me, the latter making a nest for himself up in the bow and already sketching with his coloured crayons as we travelled. Stony had the two film crew in his boat, travelling a hundred metres behind us.

It was the usual idyllic situation, like travelling down a large gutter, creamy coloured water, with coolibahs, lignum and river cooba (Acacia Stenophylla) the main vegetation. Unless you are running a big flood you mostly can't see over the banks.

A channel billed cuckoo, a bird with a very large bill, was our first interesting bird sighting. This is about the southern extent of their range, as they follow the floods down every year.

The first couple of days were uneventful; the crew filming whatever took their fancy with Serventy and Pugh the main "actors" in the doco.

On the west bank, beyond the floodplain were the sand dunes of the Simpson Desert, the Diamantina River being its south eastern boundary. To the east the sand dunes of the Strzelecki Desert.

We passed the channel leading into Andrewilla Waterhole, the largest in the Diamantina, continuing on to the ruins of the old Clifton Hills homestead.

This was originally built on a sand hill with a nice view of the river and the desert beyond, but it had a problem. Most years it was cut off for up to weeks at a time by floodwaters. It was relocated to its present site on the Gibber's, not far from Goyders Lagoon and alongside the hottest artesian bore on the Birdsville Track.

Much of the old waddy timber framework was still standing with various odds and ends lying about. The waddy (Acacia Peuce) is of interest as it is arguably the hardest timber in the world. Picking up a piece is like lifting a piece of steel and it is so dense that it doesn't make the best firewood. A protected species only found in three Australian locations. The biggest is a stand just north of Birdsville on the Bedourie Road, another large stand on Andado Station at North Bore, on the western edge of the Simpson and a number of scattered trees just south of Boulia. On average they grow to a height of about 35 to 40 feet, and look a bit like a black oak (Casuarina) that's had a bad scare – the narrow stiff leaves giving this effect.

The Birdsville Pub (which I owned from 1974-80) also had them in much of the building before the fire and refurbishment.

The mosquitoes were fairly active this trip and we were using mozzie nets on our swags. One night Stony and I had a bit of light entertainment just before we went to bed. The others had gone to bed and John had been sitting up around the fire with us. Stony and I went off to our swags and were lying in them as John decided to call it a day as well. I saw him walk briskly toward his swag with the net perfectly rigged over it. He almost made it then, suddenly stuck it in reverse and shot back toward the fire. I had been almost asleep but woke right up realising there was a bit of a "floor show" happening. John again approached his swag in a crouched position, when he reached it he went to lift up the side of the net, but decided against it once again reversing a couple of steps. Seeming to study his camp he crept toward it again with more of a purpose to his movements. He touched the net, backed off two quick steps then suddenly rushed forward and shot under it. He is a tall man and he carried out that entry with the speed of a fairy martin entering its nest. What an interesting performance – he was obviously paranoid about getting a mozzie inside his net. Made my day!

Next day we reached the huge Goyders Lagoon Swamp, the Diamantina disappears into this reappearing on the western side as the Warburton. Most years the Diamantina only reaches Goyders Lagoon Swamp, it takes a very large flood to fill this and overflow into Goyders Lagoon and the Warburton Channel, but this was one of those years.

For the sake of the film, we made a futile attempt to negotiate the swamp, spending a couple of hours pushing up narrow channels before running into mud and dead ends. The crew filmed us from the air, both in the river and the swamp. Duffy arrived in the Blitz bringing in some more fuel and gear for the crew. He was doing a fair bit of reading on this trip having lots of spare time.

The chopper had a cargo net, which we filled up with all of our gear, it took two trips. We had to deflate the boats, pulling up the wooden floors etc. When the gear was at Goyders Lagoon we were transferred in the chopper which was a nice flight across the swamp above thousands of water birds.

At Goyders Lagoon we met up with Duff again and reconstituted our expedition heading down the big lagoon and into the Warburton Channel, camping some 12kms down it. The next morning we had a very interesting experience, somewhat traumatic for Stony. The crew were hanging out of the chopper filming my boat with Cliff working on one of his drawings. The chopper was only 50 feet above us and Stony was behind me about 30m in an empty boat. Suddenly and unbeknown to the chopper pilot his Avon was blown by the down draught, bow first into a dead coolibah. The fallen tree was facing the river its leafless dead branches protruding in and on the surface of the river. The ultra hard wood was like a giant multi pronged fish spear and Stony, wrestling with the outboard was actually being pushed up into the tree, an extraordinary situation. The chopper moved away and the Avon subsided into the river with a badly lacerated bow.

I could hear Stony swearing as the chopper moved off oblivious to the drama they had caused. It took us a couple of hours and some big patches to fix the boat and it was lucky Stony wasn't staked as well.

Later that day we ran out of navigable channel as the river entered a big flood out of lignum and cane grass swamps. We had a go at getting through but I could see it wasn't going to be any good, so we made camp.

Once again we pulled the boats apart and loaded up the cargo nets to "jump" across the flood out area. This is where another interesting thing happened. As the helicopter was almost out of our sight I saw something fall out of the cargo net, dropping like a stone on to the Gibber Plain below. Pinpointing the general position we took a drive out there in the Blitz and after searching for 10 minutes found one of the swags sitting on the Gibbers, lucky there wasn't a bottle of scotch inside. We picked it up, not realising then that a second swag had fallen out, unobserved by us. We only found this out when we reached Kalamurina Station several days later. The doco producer met us there (he couldn't make the start of the trip for some reason) and was very perturbed to find that he didn't have a bed. I soon got a swag on loan from the station (Pete Dunn, the station owner loaned me one), but I still have a little smile to think of that rolled swag, sitting out on the Gibbers or Sturt Stony Desert. One day a stockman will come across it, giving him food for thought.

We were now in the main channel of the Warburton and would not expect to se the chopper again until we reached Lake Eyre.

We went only less than an hour downstream from Kalamurina homestead, when I saw broken water ahead and right across the river. We were into it before I realised the hazard and all of a sudden we had a boat full of water. I waved Stony to stop and we stepped out of the boat onto razor sharp "coral" rocks. John Manning grabbed the portable generator and began marching across this "reef" toward the other side. It seems he is sort of a natural entertainer, unconsciously providing his bit of light relief in a calamitous situation. He suddenly disappeared out of sight, except for the generator. A second later reappearing as he stepped out of the hole, hardly breaking his pace. Impressive. It took us half an hour to ferry all the gear using Stony's Avon to the northern bank.

We had blundered into a feature called Stony Crossing, a natural reef of sharp rock used by the Aborigines for centuries as a giant fish trap. In 1974, the only time a boat had been down this route, we had been many metres above Stony Crossing, riding the biggest flood in memory.

Peter Dunn later apologised for not warning me about the crossing, but it was just one of those things. It did mean some major changes to the programme however. The boat's floor was a mess of lacerated material. We spent the rest of the day camped there, mending the Avon by cutting off the blow up keeping and using it for patching material. Fortunately I had plenty of the special glue required.

However it was fortuitous in another way, Vincent and Cliff went wandering up the riverbank returning an hour later in great excitement. They had come across what turned out to be a whole lot of prehistoric crocodile teeth, which was a major find, causing great interest at the South Australian Museum.

However, their appetite for the Warburton had waned, and it was decided that they would fly in the chopper to the Lake Eyre islands, spending time there while Stony, John Manning and myself would run the river down to the lake. I thought it was a bad decision for the documentaries sake, but otherwise it certainly made my job easier.

Stony was up till the early hours of the morning finishing the painstaking job of mending the floor.

The chopper took off making two trips across to William Creek with the crew and Vin and Cliff. They would be staying there while we were travelling down the Warburton. We headed off soon after, luxuriating in all the room, towing the mended Avon behind.

We had an uneventful but very enjoyable three days travelling down the marvellous "creek". When you haven't got a camera (film crew) it's amazing how the scenery looks even greater. We caught a couple of nice yellow belly, having plenty of time for that sort of activity. We put in most of the daylight hours travelling, even though I had been down this river before, it bore no resemblance. In 1974, we were mostly travelling through the tops of coolibahs, whereas this time we were in a defined channel. I hardly saw a cliff in 1974, but this time they were visible in all their colourful splendour, the combination of gypsum, clay and sand. We had many close encounters with dingoes, as you will when they have never been shot at. One dog sat down one morning while we had breakfast – he was only about 10m away and didn't move except to scratch himself. As we moved around the fire, I told him to jump in the boat before we left, but he wouldn't be in it.

Later that day we saw a brown falcon pounce on a half grown rabbit, sitting on it as we observed it, then it flew off into a nearby coolibah and began eating it.

We reached Lake Eyre late on the third day and set up camp on the southern shore near the mouth – a very desolate place even with water flowing past, but also a fascinating place.

About mid morning the chopper came in with Vin, Cliff and the camera man and sound man for the film. For the film we made an attempt to head out into the lake along the elusive Warburton Groove, but were soon in the black mud and going nowhere.

We returned to the camp where the day was spent filming various aspects of the mouth. I showed them what I call the "Badlands" the incredibly eroded areas of clay and hard sand on the north side of the mouth, but they chose not to film it.

In the afternoon we had a very interesting flight (it took two trips with cargo nets below us) across the middle of the lake with its fascinating variety of colours to William Creek, landing alongside the little pub. Duff was already there in the Blitz to pick us up. A very pleasant and enjoyable night was spent there before heading off down the Oodnadatta Track the following day.

4

Lake Gregory – Great Sandy Desert

Lake Gregory is usually a clay-salt pan of some 300 square miles, located in the NW corner of our largest desert, the Great Sandy. In 1981 the east Kimberley region had one its biggest wet seasons on record, the Sturt Creek, that drains much of this area ran a huge and consistent flood into Lake Gregory. Consequently it filled for the first time in white man's and Aboriginal memory. The latter is evidenced by the fact that many of the local sacred sites were completely inundated. The insignificant Little Samphire Flat had become a magnificent fresh water sea of around 900 square miles.

This great natural happening passed virtually unnoticed as far as the general public were concerned I have always said that most Australians are strangers in their own country.

When I heard about it, I straight away pricked my ears up, at the time we were in the process of fitting out an ex-army Blitz truck for safari work. I had been about to take a party of bird people on another trip, but talked them into switching to a Lake Gregory safari instead.

This whole trip was written up in "Mulga Madness" but in this chapter I will give an account of our two day boat safari on the lake. By all accounts the first time boats had ever been on this brand new lake.

We had organised the necessary Aboriginal permits, and had set up a base camp on Bungabiddy Creek on the east side of the lake, not far south of the old Lake Gregory Station (now Mulan Aboriginal Community). It was a very scenic spot with a lot of small white coolibahs lining the creek. The water had backed up over seven kilometres and was well up into their branches of many of them.

It was an ideal base camp, particularly for an ornithological party. The birding was quite good (land based birds) around the camp, and back up the creek into the desert country, good local rains meant the country was covered in feed and plenty of wildflowers coming along (it was May).

I had arranged to charter the Balgo community's aircraft for a fly over the lake, and a few of us did this on the first morning. It was a spectacular sight from the air. You wonder where else in the world such a phenomenon can occur and go pretty well unnoticed.

A couple of good sized "islands" claimed our attention; these consisted of a few large isolated sand dunes with the tops still out of the water. As we flew over one of these, we spotted hundreds of nesting birds. On closer inspection they were the large caspian tern. We estimated around 1,000 nests, which later turned out to be the largest caspian tern colony ever recorded.

We were to stay nine days in the Lake Gregory area, and the next week was spent operating short boat trips of a few hours duration mostly in the creek and along the shore lines, making sure all 18 people in the party spent plenty of time on the water.

My old mate Eric Worrell (Gosford Reptile Park), and the first man to "milk" taipans for their venom) was busy filling his suitcase full of long sleeved shirts with various reptiles. We did a few trips in the vehicles with the local Aboriginal people. The women were very adept at locating the snakes, most of which were hibernating at this time of the year. They would dig them up, but as they came close to them, they would give loud shrieks of laughter and jump back from the hole. Eric would then dig the last bit, grab the hibernating snake and put it in his "snake bag". Later, back at camp he would transfer it to a shirt sleeve and put it in the old suitcase. This same suitcase would be later booked through as general luggage from Adelaide to Sydney! I don't know if nowadays that would constitute a terrorism threat or not.

On one long day trip we were returning from the closest island when we came across a lone dead mulga tree with a two metre long black headed python draped around its branches. Stony is a keen snake catcher and I don't mind pythons, so we decided to catch it for Eric, who had stayed with the camp party. Both boats converged on the tree from different directions, much to the consternation of most of the party. My wife Patti threatened to divorce me, and Brian Crisp was sitting so far up the back of the punt, as to be mostly out of it! Stony managed to grab the python by the neck, while I distracted its attention. As it thrashed around a fair bit putting it in a bag was no easy task and that wasn't the end of it. The crew had just begun to settle down a bit, when the python suddenly reared up in the middle of the punt giving everyone attacks of hysterics. There were numerous gasps and squawks and I heard someone mutter "they think they are bloody Harry Butler!" The snake had come out through a hole in the bottom of the bag. We had to catch it all over again, and this time we tied the hole off as well. During all of this pantomime the python never attempted to bite us.

After we had been at our base camp for four days, seven of us set off in the two boats for an exploration of one of the larger islands. Stony was the other boatman, and my youngest daughter Kate was also on board.

We headed the two kilometres down Bungabiddy Creek, and out on to the massive desert sea, setting a course for the closest island, a distance of 16 kilometres. The water was quite calm and we reached the "island" several hours later. The "island" was really a number of desert sand hills located on higher ground. It was well covered with clumps of mulga trees, smaller acacias, sennas etc. and plenty of grass and herbage. In other words, a typical part of the Great Sandy Desert enjoying a good season. The difference lay on the edges and in the air, there were birds everywhere! We could see the tracks of feral cats and dingoes stranded on the island. The lower part of the shoreline had become swamp areas with many different species such as dotterels (plover) and plovers (lapwing) nesting.

This island was seven kilometres long, and after an excellent day's birding, we headed off down the other end to camp. In places it was impossible to travel through the inundated bush near the shoreline because of the masses of orb spiders and their webs, and we were forced into the open water.

We made camp on a sand spit on the extreme southern end of the island it was a lovely setting as the sun set into the lake. I hopped in the boat with Kate, and we rowed out a bit from the camp. The water was coloured with reds and golds from the setting sun and the campfire back on the spit looked particularly welcome. After the meal I talked to Bill on the radio, some 24 kilometres distance. Lying in my swag that night, I couldn't think of anywhere else that I would rather be.

Next morning the birds woke us in particular a pair of swans just offshore, who were studying our camp with interest. We had a good breakfast of bacon and eggs and headed off to complete our navigation of the island. Very soon we came across around a dozen swans' nests, large mounds of vegetation floating in shallow water. Most contained eggs.

After a while the shore line became very indistinct, as there were hectares of floating water weed. The island had flattened out with no sand hills in sight, so I decided to climb a tree for a look around. We tied up to a healthy looking mulga, which the floodwater had not yet killed. With my new Lietz binoculars around my neck, I climbed the tree to a height of about three metres above the water. After I had a look around and worked out our best route, I shifted my position for a better look. I've climbed a lot of trees in my time, and I was standing on what I reckoned was a good solid looking branch, next thing there was a sound like a pistol shot, and I speared into the lake, still peering through the binoculars! As my feet touched bottom I remembered thinking "I know how deep the water is here". In fact it was over two metres and I came spluttering to the surface alongside my floating hat, still holding the binoculars but without my specs. Stony yelled, "stand still" and dived out of the boat into the lake. I felt him scratching around my feet like a sand crab, and then he appeared wearing a pair of specs! He asked if they were mine – I said they would do, and we both got back into our boats, both of which were rocking with the laughter of their occupants.

Soon we struck shallow water and very thick floating weed, so we had to walk behind and push the boats, or walk in front and tow them with a rope. The outboard motors could be used some of the time but for the most part Stony and I, and sometimes the whole party had to walk. We were about ready for lunch by the time we reached the northern end of the island. The day was quite warm so we boiled the billy in the shade of a luxuriant coolibah tree, on a rise overlooking the lake. The floating weed looked for all the world like dairy pasture in the south. How would the scene appear in 10 or 20 years time? Probably the same as it did 10 or 20 years earlier. A harsh salt lake with the odd sand hill, mulga and samphire flats. Such is nature. That evening we arrived back at camp across a dead calm lake, much richer for our experience.

As I write this (2003), Lake Gregory has once again filled, and still holds a lot of water. In 2002 while on a 4WD Canning Stock Route safari, I detoured for a camp on the west side of the lake, and a memorable camp it was.

5

Cooper Creek – 1974 and 1990

The 1974 floods enabled me to operate some desert boat expeditions that I have only ever dreamed about. They were the biggest inland floods in white man's memory, causing Lake Eyre to fill. I will simply give a brief summary here (with the exception of our Lake Eyre crossing) of the two Cooper Creek boat trips, as they were written up in my first book "Bush Safari" (Rigby 1980). Previously the only boat down Cooper Creek was in 1952 when Elliot Price (Muloorina Station) and Hector Brook (Clifton Hills Station) made a remarkable journey in a wooden boat from the Birdsville Track to Lake Eyre, when it contained a lot of water. They then went down the east shoreline and ended up wrecking their boat (or it fell to bits) on what is now called Brook's Island, on the southern end of Lake Eyre north. The largest island on the lake. They lived off seagulls eggs while they repaired the boat and continued on to Level Post Bay, where they were "rescued" having no radio at the time.

I made two journeys down the Cooper, in June and August of 1974, each time following the eastern shoreline down to Level Post Bay, but visiting the island locally called "Lorna's Leg", that we were the first to visit by boat in March that year.

On both occasions I had mates waiting at Level Post Bay on the bottom end of Madigan Gulf. On the first of these a mate and I spent a night in the Koppermanna Swamp with five women, unable to make land in time, a memorable occasion!

In 1990 the Cooper was once again a massive river, pouring its waters into Lake Eyre. I was set to go as usual with a party of six.

There were three boat men and my eldest daughter Georgina, 10 in all, I had my old ex SAS Zodiak and Avon inflatables, plus a '12ft keeled tinny'. We also towed a small rubber duck carrying extra fuel.

Our take off point was near Etadunna Station where the floodwaters came out of the Koppermanna Swamp. We were travelling in my International Acco Blitz safari truck and Malcolm Mitchell from Muloorina Station was there to take it back to the station, so that he could pick us up after the trip. I allowed 10 days to get down to Lake Eyre and back to an old oil "shot line", to be picked up, a distance of around 190kms.

Our party was a mixture of farmers, a stockbroker, city secretary and an English butler doing the British bit for wealthy Australian businessmen. This bloke had bought 96 rolls of 36 exposure film, so he obviously liked taking the odd shot.

As usual the camp before departure was about staff getting gear organised, and the party getting accustomed to the idea of what they were embarking upon. Five of them were friends, knowing each other prior to the trip.

Next morning with fully loaded boats, we set out through the big swamp, winding our way between the coolibahs and lignum. I had crossed this swamp a number of times before, but landmarks were conspicuous by their absence.

I followed as well as I could, a set course, which would bring me out where a small channel would take us from the swamp into the main channel of the Cooper. It seemed to be the only exit from the swamp.

We had lunch on small sandy spit and kept on. I had organised for video batteries to be delivered to Etadunna. The owner, Paul Broad, was going to fly over in his Cessna and drop them to us if they arrived. About mid afternoon while I was trying to locate the very elusive channel, we heard the drone of an aircraft and Paul Broad came in sight. He dropped the well-padded blue plastic package surrounded by foam for flotation. It hit the water nearby (too "nearby" some would have said!) and we retrieved it, the recipient being pretty impressed with the Birdsville Track service.

Paul Broad did a circuit then let me know on the UHF radio that the channel was about half a kilometre away. That saved time and we were soon in the narrow channel, snaggy with fast flowing water. I was towing the little yellow "duck" and became snagged on a bend, threatening to dump the fuel in the river. Fuel drums were tied in but still better inside than out. Stony who was behind me, jumped out of his boat and levered the rubber duck off the snag. He had water up to his chest and had a fair bit of trouble doing it. Water was nippy too, but that wouldn't have worried Stony. After 10 minutes or so we saw the big red sand hill that marked the main Cooper channel, we pulled in there. It was a good camp, looking out over a forest of coolibah and lignum, everyone being in a high state of excitement and anticipation.

There are few places in the world where such an adventure is possible.

Next day we headed down a river averaging 150m wide with coolibah both sides. This is the little known Tirari Desert, our most arid next to the Simpson. It borders Lake Eyre on the east, south and western sides, the Warburton River its north eastern boundary with the Simpson to the north of that. Mostly a dune desert coloured off white, yellow and red, with "satacite" salt lakes becoming more predominate as you near Lake Eyre.

A perfect day with a good current. Let the boats drift for a few sections just enjoying the silence and birdcalls. George shot five ducks that we cleaned up for dinner that night. Then we came across a few small islands that were active with rabbits. We pulled up and Stony jumped off, ran one down and wrung its neck. They had eaten the island out and were in pretty poor condition. We despatched a dozen doing themselves and the country a favour. Kept a few of the fatter ones for the pot. Saw a lone camel on a sand hill in the distance and he seemed as interested in us, as we were with him.

Birdlife as usual was ever present, but there was a lack of genuine "ornithologists" in this group.

Over the next couple of days we saw a fine looking brumby stallion stranded on an island. Still plenty of feed so he would have got off okay. Saw several others as well, plus the same camel that seemed to be following us. We gradually ran out of coolabahs, with just the odd one now and then, providing a welcome relief to the landscape.

A bit of wind this time of year, and our third night out found us in a nice little inlet well protected from the wind. Main drama that night was when the other boatman (Crabby) lost his multi grips. These are prized and valuable tools for us. Actually there was another drama earlier on.

I was rummaging in my bag (a regular past time) looking for one of my Nikon lenses. I sort of inadvertently flicked it out. It landed on the side of the boat, and then rolled into the river. Georgi, quick as a flash plunged an arm into the water, touching it but not able to save it. My cameras live a hazardous existence.

A lazy lunch on a sand hill and George as usual had gone to sleep with his hat over his eyes. We quickly packed up, got in the boats and drifted off leaving George in splendid isolation. We went around a bend then landed and headed back to the lunch camp watching behind the sand hill. Poking our heads up we watched George and after a couple of minutes he woke up and sat up. He looked casually around him and seeing the place deserted just gave a little chuckle. Big anti-climax.

An early start with a long day through one of the world's most desolate landscapes. This was somewhat softened by a fair coverage of poached egg and yellow top daisies, a result of good earlier rains.

About 4.30p.m. we reached what I call the Cooper broad water, a sheet of water two to three kilometres wide in places, before the Cooper runs into Lake Eyre. We went through the Cooper mouth into Australia's inland sea, always a heady sensation and something a very small number of people have experienced. I think it compares equally with climbing Ayers Rock and one thing in its favour is it doesn't upset the locals.

There is a small island of several acres right at the Cooper mouth. In the big floods of 1974 and on the first of my two trips down the Cooper, I buried two five gallon drums of boat fuel. I dug them up, or what was left of them which wasn't very much. There was just the rim of one drum and the wire handles, plus a pile of rust. The salt had done its work. In 1974 I had intended to completely circumnavigate the lake and this was to be one of the fuel dumps. '74 was the one year where such a trip could have been possible, but in the end it became too hard. It would have taken three to four weeks and I had trouble getting a crew to participate. It wouldn't have been a very pleasant trip with lots of shallow water walking in black mud, with the scenery alternating from mirages to the most desolate on earth. The one time Lake Eyre is truly exquisite is when there is no wind (rare) in the early morning and late evening. If you have clouds for a sunset, that is a bonus. Some of my most memorable sunsets have been on Lake Eyre.

It was an idyllic camp that evening, but no clouds for a sunset. We headed out on to the lake for over a kilometre but kept digging up mud and returned to camp. One thing you can do on Lake Eyre is walk on unlimited beaches and that was a popular past time. A few red capped dotterals, crows and silver gulls were about the extent of the birdlife on this occasion.

Next morning we headed back through the Cooper mouth, past the island and into the "broad water", however the wind had blown a lot of the water to the other side and we were bottoming a fair bit. Roger, Bill, Tim and Keith walked along a peninsula about five kilometres, which lightened the load and made it easier. On the second day up river we were having bets on when we would reach the shot line when we would finish, and Roger won that little competition. Up ahead we could see the Blitz and a couple of other Muloorina four wheel drives, with Malcolm and the boys ready to pick us up.

We loaded up and began the slow trip south to Muloorina.

OCTOBER SAFARI

I had another small party waiting for another trip, if I judged the water levels sufficient to allow it without too much risk of a stranding. Some of my judgements are made on what might be described as "doubtful data", but I don't have much option. If water levels are holding, or dropping only inches in the duration of a trip, I then try to get a few reports from up river, even as far as Queensland. I have often tried estimating how long the tail end of a flood might take to reach my area of operation, but they are just "educated" guesses based on my own experience. I value reports from the handful of station people living on the river, but no two floods are ever the same. The most complex and unpredictable part of the Cooper is between Innamincka and the Birdsville Track. This is a massive wilderness of channels, lignum and cane grass swamps, flood flats, lakes and waterholes. When you fly over this region of the Strzelecki desert during a big flood, there can be water from horizon to horizon, as was the case in 1974. In lesser floods it is an outback paradise of full waterholes, lakes, swamps etc with a great explosion of birdlife, particularly if the desert has enjoyed good rains as well. This of course means one of the world's greatest displays of wild flowers. Over the years I have operated many 4WD vehicle and camel safaris in this region during and after floods. It is the very essence of outback Australia, offering the best of firewood (coolibah), the best fresh water fish in the world (yellow belly and black bream), perfect travelling for camels, and a feast of birdlife. It was in this region in 1979 that one of my camel expeditions (which included the late Shane Parker, curator of birds from South Australian Museum) rediscovered the rare night parrot, an incredibly exciting moment.

The reason that I have not run boat safaris in this region of Cooper Creek is that the channels are intermittent. A motorised boat expedition may have been possible in 1974, but I was too busy doing other things. In the early 90's Dennis Bartel (on his own) navigated the area by canoe with the aid of air drops, which was no mean feat.

So, in October, with a small party of three, and a good mate of mine from Burra called Matt Riley, we headed once more up to the Cooper. This time I only had my old Zodiak, which was roomy enough to take the five of us and our gear. I did include another smaller four cylinder Yamaha outboard as a spare; our main motor was the ever-reliable 15hp two stroke Yamaha.

Malcolm Mitchell was once again at the Cooper to meet us, and returned to Muloorina with my vehicle. This small party was in stark contrast to the trip of a few months earlier. Just a few of us, one boat and quite hot weather around the 38 degree celsius mark.

It was basically an uneventful safari. Because of more daylight hours and fewer people, we had much earlier camps. When we were beyond the timberline, most of our lunch camps saw us with a large orange beach umbrella raised above our small lunch table. Looked unsympathetic with the landscape but made our shadeless lunch camps very pleasant.

At every opportunity we would jump in the river, a past time that never loses its appeal, Matt tried unsuccessfully for callop or bream, but they simply were not biting at this time. The canvas canopy on the boat made travelling on the water very pleasant, but I was getting a bit concerned with the falling water levels. This was very definitely my last trip with this flood.

My party consisted of a young lady called Cindy whose main interest was in obtaining a very dark tan. Then there was Bruce Dawson, a young trainee pilot, getting a look at the real bush. He was also pretty interested in Cindy. The third party member was an ex-union representative, school teacher turned writer called Brian Sheedy. He had written several useful in depth handbooks on outback travel and was indulging in a bit of extraordinary travel in this instance.

Matt was an ex-station man, now living in Burra, who I would describe as a bushman /businessman/contractor, not to mention all round good bloke, and a great student of the human condition.

He got his monies worth one night at my expense. It was a hot, humid night with the possibility of a thunderstorm. A night I would prefer to forget. It started out okay, as I lay on top of my swag, just about to nod off, when I felt dozens of tiny bodies invading my person. They were the formidable "pissants", the smallest of the species. With a curse I dragged my swag some metres away shook it out and tried again. Ten minutes later they were at me again. I could hear Riley chuckling to himself, which didn't improve my demeanour. In all, I had four shifts and when I was overrun yet again on the fourth, I did my block properly with a curse or three. I chucked the whole bloody swag in the river, seeking to drown the little bastards. By this time Matty was rolling around in his antless swag consumed by mirth.

I dragged my various swag components from the river and hung them over the boat canopy, and then I jumped into the river to get rid of a few hangers on. I then had to boil the billy while I waited for my swag to dry out a bit, and at this stage brother Riley decided to join me as there is never too many cups of tea in his day. I ended up getting a couple of hours sleep free of my tormentors, out in the spinifex away from the river. Normally we have very little trouble from ants.

Thunderstorms in the region gave us some dramatic cloud formations, and most nights we had marvellous sunsets. I have observed my share of these wonderful concoctions of nature, both in Australia and overseas. Surely nowhere else in the world are they as consistently spectacular as inland Australia. When there was no wind or breeze (most evenings) the mirror like waters of the Cooper would try and outdo the sky with reflections as good as the real thing. You really have to be "out there" and "doing it" to reap the real benefit of these sky shows, sitting in some lodge, luxurious or otherwise, will only ever deliver a second best experience. I have seen some great displays in the tropics, but have to say that nothing can equal the desert sunsets.

After a number of lazy days we reached the Cooper mouth and camped for the better part of a day on the little desolate treeless island. Later in the morning a fox gave us some entertainment. It walked up to within 20 feet of us and proceeded to eat the carcase of a smoked chicken I had discarded. Although not mangy, it wasn't in real flash condition, so the carcase was a great prize. It finally headed off down the other end of the island; it had presumably been marooned by the floodwaters, evidenced by its poor condition. Being a fox, I should have shot it, but couldn't bring myself to abuse such trust. Must be getting soft. The dingoes keep the fox numbers down and we were seeing and hearing plenty of them.

Next day we sailed out to the lake before running out of water. We camped on the Lake Eyre beach that night speculating that it was possibly the longest stretch of uninterrupted beach in the world. Just an idle thought.

As usual it was interesting to observe the ongoing competition between the two dominant scavengers, the crows and the silver gulls. The gulls won out every time.

In the morning we got away early putting in three long days back to our oil shot line rendezvous with Malcolm Mitchell. I was a bit concerned with getting stranded, and on a number of occasions it was all hands pushing the Zodiak through water several inches deep.

That was the last time I was down the Cooper in boats. Since 1990 there hasn't been a flow across the Birdsville Track. I am writing this chapter from my camel camp on Kings Creek Station in the Northern Territory. It is mid February and we have just received a steady four and half inches of rain and there are reports of good falls across the inland. Maybe this is the worst drought in memory finally coming to an end, and once again the Cooper will justify its reputation as one of the world's truly unique waterways, and pour its "white" waters into the inland sea that is Lake Eyre. If it does, I will be ready to undertake another series of inland voyages. Definitely one of my favourite pastimes.

6

The Magic Carpet

The "Magic Carpet" operation evolved in a rather curious fashion.

When I was living on Kangaroo Island in the 1980's a bloke by the name of Anthony Willoughby contacted me from Tokyo. He ran a business called "I Will Not Complain International". He told me that it involved taking small parties of American executives on adventurous journeys all over the world. All these prospective clients had to join his "I Will Not Complain" Club, which meant that prior to embarking on the trip they would each sign a form stating that under no circumstances would they ever complain – no matter what!

He wanted to come over and check out my operation, so a couple of weeks later, he and his wife arrived on the island. They spent three days with Patti and me, which included an overnight camel trek up the Ravine de Casoars and along the spectacular 800 feet cliffs at the back of our farm. We did a lot of talking, and at the end of the time he offered me a very lucrative contract.

He wanted me to put an 11 day itinerary together that included as many different adventures as possible. I might add that Anthony was an Englishman who had been raised in Africa. It sounded like he had a pretty interesting childhood, which is why it surprised me somewhat when he requested that there be no danger to his group. I was a bit non-pulsed by this, because I thought he would have known that true adventure must necessarily include an element of danger. This request was added; as he and Virginia were about to board their aircraft back to the mainland.

I thought about this for a couple of days and then I gave his partner and financial backer (an American called Guy Cihi) a ring. I mentioned my dilemma, and talked about a couple of fairly radical ideas I had for the trip. He just said, "Go for it man – consider it done", and that settled that.

This was back in the gold old days before all the disgusting un-Australian litigation began rearing its mediocre head.

I began planning the trip. It would consist of a three day raft trip on the River Murray, living off the land. We would drive in my old "Blitz" through the north east pastoral country (semi desert) to the Flinders Ranges, where we would do some gold prospecting. From there a three day camel trek, before going across to the world's longest salt lake (Lake Torrens) for a short boat trip around the southern end. A chopper would then fly in a chef with a gourmet meal, do some flights with the party before we returned to Adelaide.

This trip was a big success and is written up in my last book (Ten Thousand Campfires) and called "I will not complain". The point of mentioning all this is that at the end of the trip, I was left with this massive raft measuring 21 feet by 16 feet – a packing case top, steel two inch pipe frame, with eighteen 44 gallon drums for flotation. A mate of mine (Ralph Ohlmeyer) in the river town of Waikerie had organised the building of it, 'helped by a mate of his, Robert Hart'.

It had been left on the riverbank at Nikalapko Station where another mate, the manager (Rob Langley) was keeping an eye on it.

On my 50th birthday, I had a floating dinner party, formal from the waist up that happened to fall on a very hot Australia Day where there was a fair bit of traffic on the river. All 12 of us had swags intending to roll them out on the bank about midnight.

We began with only a beer each, but then about an hour later a speedboat arrived from the Commercial Hotel in Morgan, loaded to the windscreen with grog and tucker.

When midnight came we didn't see any reason to pull into shore and one by one people rolled their swags out on their floor as we drifted through the night.

About four in the morning there was a hell of a noise and we came to a halt. We had drifted into a dead gum tree and there we stayed until breakfast.

After boiling the billy and a long lazy breakfast, we took to the river again until we reached Nikalapko Station, passing the land Patti and I would buy and move to in a year or so.

One interesting "incident" that occurred through the night – we had thought of everything but coffee and about 10p.m., spotted a houseboat moored with one dim light showing. We were able to manoeuvre ourselves so that we would drift into the side of it (the raft had buffers of old tyres around the sides). We did so, and heard a couple of frightened exclamations from inside the houseboat. I made a formal request for coffee, preferably not instant; the only reply I received was the sound of every lockable window and door on the houseboat being locked!

They were probably a young honeymoon couple and we had put the fear of death into them. We probably appeared to them in the dark as a great "blob" with a crowd on it – like a houseboat that had gone under a very low bridge. So, it was a dinner party with everything except coffee.

I kept thinking about the possibility of an ongoing commercial operation with the raft, so decided on a week long float down the river with Patti, to consider it further.

It was the mid nineties. And the Murray was flooding, which is a bit of a bloody novelty as I write this. Anyway, we drove up to Morgan and out to Nikalapko with a bit of gear. Rob helped us get it into the river with the aid of a tractor and some lengths of pipe, because it weighed around a tonne.

Patti hadn't been all that keen on this trip for some reason, but we finally pushed off. Straight away, we were swept under some low hanging red gum branches, and some of the framework broke a limb. Next thing Patti was hit on the shoulder by something which bounced off, rolled across the raft and into the river. It was an unused mud nest of a murray magpie – it must have hurt and Patti was annoyed threatening to jump off there and then. However we were not close enough to the bank for such a terminal manoeuvre, and soon broke through into the open water. As Patti's shoulder improved, so did her disposition, and there was no more talk of mutiny.

We had a very relaxing and entertaining six day trip floating around 200kms to Walker Flat. Both Georgi and Kate (our daughters) and friends, plus another mate and his daughters joined us for a couple of days, but for the most part we were alone. The flooding river meant that we only encountered one houseboat that was travelling and had the river practically to ourselves.

The commercial venture was still taking shape in my head, when I had a phone call from an irate shack owner at Walker Flat saying that the raft was "pouring oil into the Murray". Well a tiny bit of oil can sometimes look like the wreck of the Valdez, but I had to do something about it. I rang up three mates (Bill Oliver, Fred Osmond and Ian Wright) and we headed over to Walker Flat, the idea being to float the raft down to Mannum, here I would cut it in two, and transport it up to the start of the Murray. There it would be reborn as the "Magic Carpet".

The three of us (after fitting a new 44 gallon drum) headed off on a very enjoyable two day trip, spending the one night travelling about 12kms. The next morning we quietly pulled into a shack of a mutual mate of ours, a bloke called "Scotty" from Willunga. He was fast asleep in his bed, and I crept in and twisted his big toe. After a smoko there we headed off down the wide river, doing a bit of fishing and enjoying a beer. I saw something approaching with speed, making a large bow wave. Fred picked up the binoculars gave an oath, and immediately crawled under a large tarp. He had had this particular problem before and wanted no part of this one.

It was a boat inspector, in a deadly looking boat that would have been more at home patrolling our northern coastline keeping out drug smugglers and illegal immigrants.

The "driver" was a magnificent looking specimen in an immaculate uniform complete with peak cap and a very expensive pair of shades. He circled us once like a great white positioning itself for the kill. Three pairs of eyes swivelled around, mesmerised by this obvious "predator".

He pulled up next to us switched off his twin Yamahas and remarked "What have we here?" I took it as a serious question, and said "just four er, three blokes, floating down the Murray, enjoying a fish and having a beer".

I don't think it was the answer he was after. In fact I don't think he wanted an answer. Then the interrogation began. "Do you have a boat licence?" I was about to say no, because I didn't at the time, doing most of my boating where I am the only one there. Then Ian said, "I do", and dug his out, much to my relief, he peered for a long time at the raft, and then seemed to give a shiver of disgust. There was probably nothing like it in his book of rules, so he fixed his attention on the Avon. "Is it registered?" "No" I said. "Has it got an anchor?" "No," I said. "Has it got a fire extinguisher?" "No" I said. "Has it got a torch?" "Yes," I said, "Matter of fact I've got a couple," I said, feeling quite please with myself.

He went quiet for awhile, and seemed to be weighing the whole situation. We all (including Fred) waited with baited breath. "Look," he said," You had better get this Avon registered as soon as you get home." I said that I would.

"Now, you blokes are going straight into the shore, aren't you?" he said. I didn't catch his drift and started to say no, we were going on down to Mannum (about five kilometres away) when he cut me off and said forcefully, "You're going straight into shore aren't you?" To which I replied hastily "Yes, we're going straight into shore."

With that he gave us a smile and a wave, looked at the raft shaking his head, and took off to take on more predictable prey. Not a bad sort of a bastard, we reckoned, including Fred as he re-emerged from the tarp.

We gave the raft a bit of a nudge with the Avon, getting down to Mannum as quick as possible, not wanting to push our luck.

Now the thing is, you can't just leave something like our raft in a built up area and this was on my mind as we wouldn't be able to split the raft for almost a year. As we drifted into Mannum I noticed a few small islands literally choked with willows. They formed a sort of boundary between the river and a big backwater. We ducked over in the Avon, and pronounced them perfect for our purpose, so pushed the raft across. We were able to completely push it in under the willows, so as to be unseen from the road or anywhere else. We had to do a few "shuttles" with our gear across to the shore, where Patti was due to pick us up. So ended that little voyage.

In 1993 I was ready to do our first 16 day "Magic Carpet" Murray River raft trip.

A long time mate of mine (who had worked on the first Cape York 4x4 safari in 1969 and many others since) called Duffy Sigston and Bill Oliver drove over to Mannum with the Avon on top of the Toyota. We motored over to the willow island and found the raft as we had left it with the addition of a few kilos of cormorant droppings. We pulled it out and pushed it the short distance across to the Mannum Caravan Park, where we had arranged with the proprietor to do the work.

We took the timber off the frame and cut the pipe framework up so that it could be loaded on to the Blitz. It took us half a day, but we finally loaded everything up and took it all back to McLaren Flat. It was later delivered to a trucking depot, and accompanied by Duffy it travelled by semi trailer over to Albury, the large town up the top end of the Murray River. This was the most practical place to begin this operation. Duff had a big job – he had to get the raft re-assembled and fitted out with new drums by the time I arrived to start the trip.

I duly headed off in the Toyota from my property at McLaren Flat, taking a long day to drive along the Murray to Albury. I pulled up at the Railway Hotel, where we were all staying prior to the trip.

I finally located Duff, and the news wasn't good. He had not been able to get the work done for a number of reasons. He needed to hire a portable welder to do the work on the riverbank. One wasn't available on the day he needed it, which meant our job was put well behind. In addition their forklift (the transport company who had agreed to help us) had broken down, and finally, the vehicle they had agreed to hire me for Duff to pick up the drums, wasn't available. If Duff was a lesser man, he may well have shot himself.

So, the following day, we made a huge effort. The transport company went out of their way to help, and by evening we had most of the raft assembled. We worked non-stop the next day also.

About 4p.m. we rolled out the carpet, put up the canvas canopy (that covered two thirds of the raft) and drifted off the bank into a fast flowing narrow river. This was the start of a stuttering journey down the Murray that would finish when I got to the Murray mouth.

My party consisted of long time clients Eileen and Margaret Nelson, Glenda Benness and Michael Jacobs plus Duffy and I.

We swept under the bridge as we passed through Albury, causing plenty of interest as we did so. There were ominous dark clouds brewing in the west, and we pulled into the bank about 6 p.m to set up camp. No sooner had we done this than the heavens fairly opened up. It poured down, but we managed to rig a side tarp and kept pretty well dry. We had a couple of pre-dinner drinks and Michael brought out a small battery powered Christmas tree that he set up. The rain eased off, so we got a fire going and a meal on. While that was happening we set up the swags with the tarps over them. We had just finished the cooking when down came the rain again. Grabbing our plates we all scrambled back onto the raft, eating our meal with the heavy rain beating down on the tarp. We then noticed a sort of unusual situation. We had been aware of the river downstream from us gradually becoming "lighter", a sort of increasing glow. Then came the sound of a Dixieland band, and before long around the bend came an interesting sight. A large tourist paddle steamer, lit up like Lobethal over Christmas, with people hanging off it everything drowning in the heavy rain and jazz. Was a very confronting sight, and one you couldn't ignore. Five minutes later there was just the rain and the night – and us.

It rained all night and everyone kept dry. We woke up to a beautiful morning with the birds singing, and a river ready to take us to goodness knows where.

Compared to the Murray that I am used to, this one was a very narrow active waterway, only averaging 40 or 50 metres wide, and often a far bit narrower. The thing about these raft trips is – you know where you are going to start, but have no idea where you are going to finish, it depends on the speed of the river. The furthest we ever travelled in the 10 days was 170kms, and the shortest trip was 65kms on a slow river. This chapter deals with various highlights and incidents that have occurred on these trips over the past 13 years or so.

Our inaugural trip was getting away to a flying start, with no opportunity to read books. The river was full of snags and Duff and I were often in and out of the inflatable, pushing the raft around the worst of them, and getting us around the sharp bends, before we ploughed into the bank. I had perfected a very efficient way of manoeuvring the ponderous craft around bad obstacles and into shore. A metre long rope ties the Avon to the centre of the rear of the raft; the rope fastened to the raft through the middle of one of the tyre buffers. When manoeuvring is required, we drive the boat up against the tyre, and if a big or quick manoeuvre is required, someone has to press down on the front of the inflatable, to keep it from "rearing up". By using the power of the pivot, we push the raft, which ever way is required. Sometimes, to get out of trouble, we put the outboard in reverse and do a rotation of the raft to avoid a hazard. I have got this method down to a practised art, but now and then we come unstuck.

Little snags, we don't worry about, but a big snag usually has one of these effects – the worst scenario is we "pop a drum" and that can be quite spectacular. On one occasion a drum shot out from the side row, flying about 20 feet in the air. Sometimes they are reusable, sometimes not. We always carry a spare on board, but the raft is capable of floating on half the number it uses. On other occasions we get locked on to a snag, and can be up to an hour getting off a bad one. Other times there's just a loud bang and we float off, but in general the big ones are to be avoided.

Even so, on the first trip we sometimes went for up to half an hour without starting the motor and that is what the operation is all about – the sounds of silence.

On the third day we came into a little river town called How Long, and a couple of interesting things occurred here. I made the mistake of asking a resident "How Long" he had been there. He stormed off, calling me a smart arse, so I worked out that the resident must have long tired of strangers asking that one – and fair enough. It's a bit like a number of people we get on and around our camels, asking whether the bulls have to be "bricked" to make them go, yeah we get a bit jack of that one too.

The other thing that happened in How Long was that Michael suddenly said, "I'm off". I wasn't sure if he meant he was going bad, on the nose or what, but it seemed he had had enough. He reckoned he was a man of action, and that the operation was too slow for him. Fair enough, I thought, particularly as we didn't want to argue about a refund. So, the last we saw of Michael was getting onto a coach en route to Sydney. You never know with some people.

After we had left Albury, an ostrich carrier in Yarrawonga by the name of Ray Waygood (known locally as the "Rusty Ballbearing") had been organised to bring my troop carrier back to Yarrawonga, as I anticipated finishing somewhere around there.

The first trip was pretty exciting at times due to the fast flowing meandering narrow river, which at times meandered so much that it was only a few hundred metres or less to walk across the land – to travel the distance on water would take an hour or so.

On one occasion we were swept under some low hanging gums and we lost our Australian flag and had our canopy flattened. We didn't react quite quick enough, because that canopy was designed so that for eventualities such as that, we could pull the bottoms of all four legs out (they were each mounted on blocks of wood and guyed with ropes) and "collapse" the structure. Putting it up in a minute after the hazard was behind us. In this case we had a bit of repair work to do.

There was virtually no river craft on this section of river from Albury to Yarrawonga. Larger boats including houseboats didn't often go past the Yarrawonga Weir. We did see a number of fishermen in tinnies, and one of our regular amusements was noting the reaction of some of these. The Magic Carpet was a sight to see as it swept around a timbered bend, and was often upon the fisherman before they realised it.

On one occasion a bloke was fishing on a log about one and half metres high, and when we were all of a sudden on him, and I said ""How are you going mate?"" he actually fell arse over head into the undergrowth. A bigger show than hooking a large cod he reckoned, and took it quite well.

We often had a line in, but only hooked a few small callop as well as carp on that occasion.

I had made arrangements for another mate called Malcolm Hansen to meet us about half way through the trip. He jumped on a coach, then got a ride out to this spot where he came aboard. He was a ranger in SA National Parks and Wildlife, and used to drive for me on occasions.

The day after we picked Malcolm up, we were heading fast down a short reach towards a bend that had a large dead river gum half way across the river. I slightly underestimated the speed and distance, and before we could get clear of it, we were swept into it, trapping us like a yabby in a net.

We laboured for half an hour, and for a while I thought we might have to go and find a cocky willing and able to pull us out with a long cable. The main problem was a thick branch that had poked itself in between about three drums. We worked on while the girls made lunch. Finally, with a combination of using an axe and bow saw underwater, and pulling flat out with the Avon, the raft was free and off down the river. It had taken us one and half hours and our worst hold up so far. But it taught me not to take the river too cheap.

Most of this country alternated between state forests of red gums and farm, mostly dairies. The bird life was good seeing some species we don't see further down the river, such as dollar birds and azure kingfishers.

After a few more entertaining days, we entered the large man-made Lake Mulwala. We followed the channel lined by large dead gums that died when the lake was flooded, and were about half way through when to my horror I saw another "official" looking boat coming. I still didn't have a boat licence due to my usual remote area activities; not knowing one wasn't required in NSW.

A similar boat to our Mannum man, with a more casual looking uniformed driver at the wheel pulled up alongside, with a cheery "How are you going?" It soon transpired that the last thing he was interested in was boat licences, registration etc. He was just interested in us as a "phenomenon"; I was going to offer him a beer, but something told me not to, lest it could be construed as a bribe or similar. He was the only officer in the newly formed Victorian River Police, based at Benalla. He said large boats were a bit of rarity upstream from Yarrawonga, and he was certainly pleased to see us.

Said he married a girl from Port Lincoln and had a lot of time for South Australians. He ended up giving us a lump of cheese and a big pile of 150,000 series river maps, which were quite a lot of use for us. He reluctantly departed after nearly an hour, heading off up river. Pity all members of the police force weren't as public friendly as he was. Reckoned he had the best job in Australia, and I didn't doubt him.

That afternoon we floated into Yarrawonga, ending up at the yacht club, where we were made very welcome. I gave the "Rusty Ballbearing" a ring and he came and picked Malcolm, Duff and I up and took us back to his trucking yard. He said he had a houseboat trailer that would take the raft out of the water (we didn't think we would survive floating over the weir!) around the weir and back on the downstream side. I have to say here that Ray was one of the most helpful people that we experienced on the river, but he definitely enjoyed a bit of drama. We were a bit taken aback when we sighted the trailer. It had three axles, but only five wheels, wasn't registered and had no indicators. That was just for starters. The timber bearers were of half rotten four by four radiata pine. All this was hastily noted by us blokes, but I just said, "thanks a lot Ray, that ought to do the job nicely". So we towed it around to the yacht club with my troopie, backing it into the water at the boat ramp and with a fair bit of trouble we managed to get it on the trailer coming out of the lake, it looked like a reluctant iceberg being taken from its natural habitat.

Out of the water it looked massive, particularly on the little trailer, and we were worried about the timbers breaking. We parked it on the immaculate yacht club lawn, and set up camp alongside it, making do with a pizza for dinner that night.

My next dilemma, was how and when to get it through the town and back into the river. If I had tried getting a permit to do the simple manoeuvre, I would have still been there 10 years later. So, I decided to do it at four in the morning.

Soon after that hour next morning we were away, sneaking along a bitumen road full of potholes in 4WD low range. As we approached the Murray Valley Highway, a bit of which we had to travel, would you believe, we saw a wide load semi coming with a house on it, escorted by a couple of civilian vehicles with flashing lights. Our good luck I thought – here's a bit of legitimacy. But was not to be when I pulled them up (they didn't like that!), the bloke in charge took one look at our "rig" and gave me a set of instructions that I won't repeat here, but in no uncertain terms informed us that we couldn't be included in their convoy. Fair enough, so we just slowly continued on our way driving through a sleeping Yarrawonga and down to the boat ramp on the river. Soon had it in the water, much to everyone's relief, including I think, the Magic Carpet's. I returned the Toyota and trailer to Ray's yard and walked back to the river. We were underway by 6.30a.m., feeling like we had done a good day's work already. This was our last day, and one of my biggest challenges at the end of each trip is to find a safe mooring for the raft. About mid afternoon I pulled up at Yarramundi Station, walked up and had a yarn to the manager. He was more than happy to keep an eye on it. It's always an all care no responsibility situation. My vehicle was brought down from Yarrawonga and we dropped the girls off there at the coach depot and drove home.

I had another party booked for the next summer, and about six weeks before departure I rang up Yarramunda Station to see how the raft was.

"It's gone," said the manager, "Some hoons cut the ropes about three months ago."

Well, there wasn't a lot I could say, so I rang the ever reliable "Rusty Ballbearing" in Yarrawonga, and he agreed to get another raft "knocked up" by my departure date. He assured me that he would get it delivered to the boat ramp on the river, as I told him the last transfer on his trailer had "cost me five years of my life" (in worry).

When I duly arrived the day before the next trip, it was finished, but still in his shed. Ray said something about me being the expert in the moving business, so I had to go through the performance again.

I am a great respecter of Murphy's Law, so this time I decided to take the bull by the horns, and make short "transfer" during the Yarrawonga rush hour, about five in the afternoon. It was an interesting 10 minutes, and I think I did age a bit more. We had a ute in front of us with its lights on, then me towing the raft on a sturdy car trailer with the flags flying, with Ray bringing up the rear with his hazard lights on, but they were faulty so only one was working. I may not have had the required permits for a wide load, but I couldn't be accused of being devious.

Into the river and it floated, which was a plus, this was an upmarket version of Magic Carpet I. It had a frame of C-Channel steel and instead of old packing cases; the floor was of smart looking 5/8" marine ply. We put our original carpet back on (this was off my sister's lounge room floor when they replaced it with a new one, and was supposed to be for my new office which was still to be built). And our canopy, which was always taken off the raft and stored separately at the end of trips.

On this occasion an old mate called Bruce Possil and a journalist from the Melbourne Age had come up to do a story on the Magic Carpet. Bruce was a freelance photographer now, but when he was on the Age had the reputation as one of the best in the business. He would go to any lengths for the photograph he wanted.

We headed off from the imposing Yarrawonaga Weir with Bruce up on top of it and the journo on board. A few days later it was on the front page of The Age in colour, an exceptional shot.

The boys camped with us that night, and did an hour in the morning before I had them picked up. Brett Armstrong and his sister, Kylie (the only others on board) and only one headed off downstream.

An interesting occurrence this trip happened an hour into the second day, we had just drifted around a bend, and there, tied up to a cliff, was the Magic Carpet I! We nudged the Magic Carpet II alongside and tied up. It was like greeting an old friend, but this was a fair bit the worse for wear. Lots of holes and gapes in the floor particularly. A steel ladder led from it up to the top of the 15 metre high cliff, so I climbed up to the top, and had a quiet look.

There was a backyard and house some 30 metres away. Checking the scene for dogs (a bit of a hazard to me in this operation when I walk into properties without a "vehicle"); I walked across and knocked on the door. A woman around 35 years of age came to the door looking apprehensive. I quickly assured her that I wasn't an axe murderer, and asked about the raft. She looked a bit embarrassed, but told me a quite credible story of how someone had rung up her husband telling to him about the raft that was marooned in a swamp nearby. He went to the area for a look at it. Then he hired a crane, got it back onto the river, and floated it to his place. He put an outboard motor on it, which was stolen the next day. From that time, they had used it as a pontoon for swimming off. Fair enough. I said they could keep it and returned down the ladder. I had put an advertisement in the local river papers, rung councils, the river police, but no-one had known a thing. It's nice to get these little mysteries solved.

Over the next five years I did a number of trips, gradually getting further down this marvellous old Murray River. Every kilometre was different. For the most part the days were uneventful, but full of ongoing delights. You have three feeds a day, a morning smoko, you constantly swim, fish, watch birds, have walks, do a lot of talking, drink a fair bit of beer on occasions, and look at some of Australia's best scenery. It's not too hard to take. Great camps on sandy beaches or upon the banks in Red Gum forests.

There are however, a few annoyances, - like water skiers when you get near town areas. I usually carry a part bag of old spuds to reinforce my right to protect my territorial waters. On occasion, skiers and speed boats would rip past close to the raft, sometimes putting water on board and wetting people's gear. I allowed them 10 metres, and if they came inside that, I would send a few spuds their way. It usually worked and they would get the message.

On this particular occasion, this ignorant skier did two close passes, showering us with water and ignoring my gestures to keep away. So, on his third run through I sent a hail of hefty spuds at him. One of them hit him on the shoulder, causing him to fall off his ski only metres from us. He was furious. It was a bit like swotting a funnel web spider, and sort of flicking it still much alive and agro into your lap. This bloke (a large tough specimen of limited intelligence) wanted to have me for dinner and tried to get up on the raft. I kept poking him off with the long handled shovel, because if he got on, I might have to get off! Anyway, his boat finally picked him up, and we drifted on quite pleased with our defences.

When the raft was in the vicinity of the town of Koondrook, I contacted an old mate of mine called Peter Disher. Peter was in his 70's and had previously done a couple of trips with us, including a Cooper Creek camel trek. He is one of the most competent ornithologists I have ever encountered with a brilliant set of eyes. Living all his life around Barham (the NSW side) on his farm, and now retired in Koondrook (Vic side) for three different raft trips, approaching and leaving his area, we had a good bit to do with him, particularly bird watching. He was a World War II digger, tough as nails, a bachelor, but lived for his birds. On the first trip he showed us something which I have valued ever since. It is the largest red gum in the world, and it happens to be on the largest island in Australia. This is Gumbower Island, many kilometres long that is literally just that. It takes a bit of finding, but the trip is most definitely worthwhile. It stands 150 feet tall, a massive tree its top sticking out well above the surrounding forest. One hundred and twenty feet up a wedge tailed eagle's nest. The average red gum grows to around 80 feet and a big one is 100 feet. I have visited this tree on a few occasions now and marvel at it, getting an almost spiritual feeling each time. One day it will no doubt be a top tourist attraction, and I am surprised it isn't already.

Sadly, Peter died in 2002, and will be missed by a lot of people.

One trip took us through the largest red gum forest in the world (Barmah Forest), together with the Millewa Forest on the NSW side; it covers a very large area. The river was high on that occasion with the water only about a foot off the top of the banks, hopefully soon to inundate the forest. Plenty of koalas in this area, some swamp wallabies, as well as the usual Western and eastern grey kangaroos. The beautiful superb parrot is also seen in this region.

There are plenty of wild pigs, and once a year the locals hold a sort of hunting orgy where they hunt the pigs with dogs, armed only with knives. Whatever turns you on, I suppose.

A mate, Alby Mangels and a mate of his called K.B. joined us on one trip beginning from the mouth of the Edward River at Picnic Point. The Edward is a big anabranch of the Murray, running up through the Riverina town of Deniliquin and back to the Murray. Albie shot a documentary for overseas viewing. Bill Oliver, his son James, my daughter Georgi and my first jack russell terrier (Trouble) were on that trip with two English tourists. Alby had enough film after about four days when he and K.B. hopped off.

On another occasion the TV programme "Getaway" shot a documentary for their series, with Sorrel Wilbey the presenter. They were only with us for three days and unfortunately little happened to make a decent doco, with one exception. Travelling through the state forest, we came across a black heifer, hopelessly bogged in the mud. A lot of the forest is leased to private landowners and it can take a bit of finding out who has cattle running there.

We pulled in and had a look. I had a couple of bush mates with me on this trip, Matt Riley and Charlie Bourne, together we rigged a rope sling using a truckies hitch, and with a fair bit of digging with the posthole shovel, we gradually winched the beast out of the ooze, which the crew duly filmed. She lay on the dry ground for about 10 minutes, then got to her feet and wobbled off. A very lucky little lady.

On a number of occasions we pushed stranded cattle and sheep back up on to the river bank. On one occasion an irate cow took exception to this and had a go at me. I was forced to take to the river.

A mate of mine from Melbourne called Darren Wallace came along as offsider on one trip, on this, we struck our lowest water ever. It was in the Swan Hill region, which is one of the shallowest parts of the Murray River. It was also the hottest trip, with some of the Murray towns recording their hottest temperatures ever. It was February 2001. The raft had been at the farm upstream from Swan Hill for two years. I just hadn't done a raft trip in that period. It was high and dry, with half the drums needing replacing. We had to spend a whole day doing this, and it was quite a job. The day was a stinker, reaching 45 degrees celsius but the farming family was very hospitable and invited my five ladies (all in their 60's and early 70's) to relax in an air conditioned room, while Darren and I got stuck into replacing the drums.

Next morning we were all ready to go and headed off. The early mornings were beautiful on the river, but there were very high temperatures predicted. In fact, we were to have a week where every day was over 44 degrees celsius, with a couple of 47 degrees celsius.

Going through Swan Hill was a problem, and we spent a couple of hours getting off great "gobs" of mud in a shallow river.

In actual fact we were handling the heat okay, the girls were living in their bathers, and we were in and out of the river all day and under the shade of the canopy. Anywhere was hot that week, but I think we might have had one of the best situations going. Even the nights were okay, being cooler nearer the water.

We were fortunate enough to see a small colony of grey crowned babblers, a bird that is becoming a lot rarer in many areas.

I needed some extra perishables and pulled in at the little township of Nyah West, and walked up the hill to the shop. I saw that it was for sale, and the more I saw of the business, the more I thought it might suit a mate of mine (David Burton, the manager of Aussie Disposals in Adelaide) who was looking to buy a business in the country. It was a licensed grocer with a post office, with plenty of room for Dave to establish a fishing/camping section.

To cut a long story short, David, Willis and family are now established there, and very much enjoying the experience. I told the original owner that if I sold it for him, he and his wife would have to do a safari with me, but I haven't seen them yet!

In the same year a small rise of water would hopefully make it possible to get through another very shallow section of river.

A dairy farmer mate from around Warnambool called Robert Crothers, who comes away with me on occasions, was offsider on this one but joining us later in the trip. Along with Roger Nutt (another regular traveller with me) and John Jones from Sydney, not to forget my little jack russell, Stubbie (son of Trouble, which was killed by a snake).

We took off from the fruit block, the couple becoming so fond of the raft as a swimming platform; they were building one of their own.

Every now and then we would strike shallow water, having to push and pull the raft over obstacles. This trip, we had a big challenge ahead, none other than the notorious "Bitch and Pups". These were a group of small islands, the "Bitch" being the larger, and the "Pups" two very small ones. Many boats had been both wrecked and stranded here over the years.

We were about six kilometres upstream from Tooleybuc and stuck fast on a gravel hump. Working for half an hour, we were not looking like getting off, when a small houseboat came along with a local farmer on board. He put a heavy rope on us, and with a lot of thrashing about, we finally came free. The next day was Australia Day and he invited us to a special breakfast that was being held on the lawns at Tooleybuc.

He also invited us to join a small flotilla of boats to make a procession into the town, starting at 8a.m.

We got going early next morning, and somehow found ourselves at the head of a varied group of around eight boats. At least we had our Aussie flag on the bock hanging off a mallee rail.

A couple of very pleasant hours were spent there, consuming a mega breakfast and talking to a lot of very nice people, one farmer ran us into his son's place to get a spare drum for the raft. One person we met was Neil Langley, a farmer and modern bullocky. His place was down near the "Bitch and Pups", and a few were giving us dire warnings of what to expect there Neil, however was a very positive bloke, and if we came "unstuck" down there said he would bring in his bullock team and pull us out. In fact, he seemed very keen on the idea. We said we would keep in touch, and finally departed Tooleybuc not anticipating lunch in any way, shape or form.

The next day we picked up the young farmer, Neil who had offered to help us through the "Bitch and Pups", and slowly approached this infamous feature mid morning. Between the "Bitch" and the Victorian side of the river was the wider, but shallower channel. It had a very rough, sharp, rocky bottom. Between the "Pups" and the NSW bank was a narrow channel about 10 metres wide with fast flowing water and many dead gum trees under the water and one right on the bend above water. It was only 150 metres through here, but it was on the bend. I could see big problems either way, but decided to go between the "Pups" and the NSW bank. I got back in the Avon and began pushing the raft as hard as I could. We were quickly in the fast current, and straight away the raft started to "spin out", heading toward the dead gum – there just wasn't enough room to manoeuvre. With a great crash both the raft and Avon were into the tree, held fast by the current. Almost immediately Neil and his mate popped their head over the "Pup" having waded across the river from the Victorian side. It was going to take more than a bullock team to get us out of this. In fact it took about an hour. By attaching two ropes to trees on the bank with truckies hitches, pulling with the Avon, pushing off with the post hole shovel, and cutting branches under water with the bow saw, we gradually inched away from the tree. Couldn't have done it without the extra men. When we were near the "Pup", we let the ropes go and I pushed like buggery with the Avon, the current spitting us back out into deeper water down stream from the "Bitch and Pups". We pulled up on the Victorian side in a nice little beach, intending to have lunch Neil had other ideas, saying that his wife had lunch prepared for us. No contest there, so the lot of us and three dogs, piled in and on to a battered little Suzuki, for a four kilometre drive to his farm where he had a number of relatives staying, and there was around a dozen of us that sat down to a very fine lunch. After lunch he said that he would harness his bullocks up to the old bullock cart and take us for a run. This proved a fascinating few hours, as we put harness on his very large, docile bullocks. I found the contrast to these and the camels very interesting. When the 10 bullocks were in harness, we headed off on a half kilometre circuit in the cart, enjoying the experience. He does presentations at some of the country shows. A lot of dedicated work, but great for people to see in this day and age. Late that afternoon he took us back and we camped on their little beach. A big day.

A couple of days later we came to the junction of the Murray and Wahcool Rivers. The Wahcool was actually the original course of the Murray. This is where I was to meet Rob Crothers, but that day Roger, John and I took off in the Avon for a trip up the Wahcool. It was fairly shallow, but we managed to get some kilometres up it before staking the Avon, something that doesn't happen too often. We patched it up, and limped back to the raft, with Rob arriving in his Toyota the following morning.

A couple of days later we had passed the Murrumbidgee junction, taking a short trip up the snag infested channel. We were having lunch the next day, when we had a little drama with my mate Stubbie. He has always been a tree climbing dog, able to get 50 feet up a gum tree, providing the branches were not too vertical.

We heard a yelp and looking up above the raft spied Stubbie 40 feet up in a river gum, standing on a large gall. He had jumped up on to the gall, but couldn't jump back down the couple of feet to a leveller section of limb. No way was he able to get down, so we put all the swags and soft gear along the bank near the water, and then rigged up a fishing rod with a wire hook. Rob and I could get about five metres up the trunk, but the next section wasn't a very good proposition. For two hours we hung on (taking in turns) to that trunk, reaching up, swinging the rod and trying to hook Stubbie's collar. A bit like trying to win the lottery and I was getting pretty worried. Finally Rob said, "bugger it" and ran up the tree like an orangutan. He reached around, grabbed Stubbie by the collar, and dropped him down to us, before sliding down himself. Would have taken a lot of guts to do that and I was very grateful.

The next night was the last and we camped on a large island at Boundary Bend. I looked around, no vertical gum trees, so I didn't worry about Stubbie, about half and hour later we were sitting around having a drink when I heard Stubbie barking but couldn't find him. We searched for 10 minutes, and then by a great stroke of luck I saw his eye peering out of a small hole in a dead spout, about 40 feet up a gum. I couldn't believe it, he must have chased a goanna up the hollow inside of the gum, and now he couldn't get down. Never a problem in four years, and now two dramas in two days! The big problem was how to get him down. There was no way we could get up there without ropes, a ladder, and a chain saw to cut him out. After a bit of thought, I rang up the local store at Boundary Bend, asking it there was a local young bloke (or girl) who was a bit of a tree climber, not so common since bird nesting has become politically incorrect. The lady said that there was a young bloke, and gave me a number. His father (on a fruit block) answered the phone and said his son was at the pictures in Swan Hill, a 100 kilometres away, but then he said, "I'm pretty good at climbing trees". It was almost dark, but he agreed to meet me on the bank half a kilometre from our camp. I went up in the Avon, and while I was discussing the problem we heard six shots in close succession, then a flashing light from my camp. You bloody beauty, I thought, he's come down. Sure enough when I returned, Stubbie was all over me like a rash. Roger had fired his .22 pistol at a spot near Stubbie, and he came down that tree like a rat out of a drain pipe. Great relief all round.

I have only ever had trouble with vandals on one occasion, apart from when the original "Magic Carpet" was cut adrift near Yarrawonga. It was downstream from Torumburry Weir, at an isolated spot in the State forest. Campers started to take the marine ply decking off, I was very thankful to the boss at Torumburry, Terry Holt, as he and one of his blokes went down and towed the raft back to a spot near the weir. Just one of the many people along the river who have given me a lot of help.

As I write this (March 2003) the "Magic Carpet" sits at Boundary Bend awaiting a rise in the river and another party. The journey down a lazy river continues, and I look forward to the next trip.

My last trip on the Magic Carpet before going to print was in March 2006. Some months earlier I had heard from Harry Borham at Boundary Bend, there had been a rise in the river and it seems some kids helped it leave its berth where it had been sitting for two years. It floated half a kilometre and became caught up on a snag, a few hundreds metres from a massive pumping system owned by a syndicate growing olives. They thought it was a threat to their pump (ridiculous view) and in their arrogance, pulled it in and hacked it to pieces with an angle grinder. Fortunately the local fisherman told Harry and he went and salvaged the marine ply decking.

So, in January, Bill Oliver and I drove up to Boundary Bend and spent three days building Magic Carpet Mark III. It was actually built in two parts, which we joined together. We had to cut up a heap of old galvanised pipe currant rack frames. These were then laid out on a concrete floor and welded together. I hadn't touched a welder for over 30 years, and found out it was like swimming – you don't forget how to do it. We then wired the original marine ply on, and this time fitted 45 gallon poly drums instead of the old galvanised 44's. All this took place in Harry's huge shed, and he and Josh (his son) were a huge help in all aspects. We eventually towed them down separately with a tractor and trailer and put them in the Murray. My old carpet had been pinched by some Polynesian fruit pickers, so I had another roll of nice second-hand shagpile for this one.

It was supposed to have been a commercial trip, but my party had to cancel last minute, so I thought – bugger it, I'll go anyway. It's an activity I very much like doing. It was going to be just me and Billycan (my jack russell) and a mate from Burra (Matt Riley) would join me for the last three days.

I drove up to Boundary Bend, camping near the raft that night. Next morning I left the Oka at Josh's place, and pushed off. There was reasonable flow, so I was making about three kilometres an hour. As I passed the giant pumps of the olive corporation, dragging tens of thousands of gallons a day out of the river, the thoughts of revenge crossed my mind, but I drifted past.

It's very pleasant travelling with a small party, but it's also very pleasant with just yourself and your dog. The silence and bird calls are occasionally interrupted when you pass an operating pump or hear a vehicle, but mostly it's the sounds of silence.

I passed a couple of fisherman in tinnies on the first day, and one had just caught a 25 pound murray cod.

Most of this trip was through State forest, and the second day I didn't see another human being, or hear one. At one stage in the afternoon an old man emu and six zebra striped chicks wandered down to the river, and I drifted to within 20 feet of them before the old bloke twigged. He jumped a metre in the air, and then ran along the bank sideways like emus can before rounding up his brood and scuttling off through the red gum forest. Later on a fine looking goshawk landed in a river coobah just metres from me, and we had a fine encounter. The raft is pretty non-threatening, except when I start up the outboard on the towed dinghy to push myself around a snag, corner or into the shore.

One morning I pushed off shore and Billy went ballistic, barking and doing laps of the raft. Kept looking at the shore, so to humour him I went to the trouble of starting the outboard and pushing the raft back into shore. Billy jumped off, ran up near the top of the bank and began digging. He'd forgotten his bone! Ran back down the bank with the bone in his mouth, and jumped on the raft, very pleased with himself. Never a dull moment with jack russell's.

Most afternoons Billy and I would pull up at a good sandbar and go for a walk in the bush, and we would have our daily swim, usually at lunch time.

After lunch on the fourth day I arrived at the old Yungra Station homestead, where I had arranged to meet Matt. I tied up and walked up steps to be met by John Tate, the present owner. He and his small son were as interested in the raft as I was in the old homestead, and we had a cup of tea, Matt arriving an hour later.

Leaving his ute there, we headed off downstream, it had been a very enjoyable four days on my own, but I was very pleased to have Matt on board.

We intended to drift day and night for the rest of the trip. It's always an entertaining experience.

We pulled into shore in some particularly fine red gum forest, lit a fire and put on some steaks. Just on dusk we pushed off, drifting down a carpet of colour. A particularly good sunset coloured both the sky and river, and nothing could have been more peaceful with only the muted call of an owlet nightjar breaking the silence.

We eventually rolled our swags out, away from the edges so that a snag wouldn't wipe us off through the night, and went to sleep. Now, every night is "interesting" when you're drifting on a raft, and this one was no exception. We hit the bank a couple of times, but each time the raft just spun off slowly and continued on. It was just before midnight when engine sounds were noticed, and as we drifted on they became louder and the river became illuminated by bright lights. I could see through my field glasses that two machines were working. As we drifted closer we could see a very large pumping complex was being installed. There were three men present, two driving front end loaders. We were unobserved as the overhead lights must have prevented them seeing us. It looked like they were working like buggery to get it all installed before daylight, like they were guilty. Probably not, but it seemed a peculiar situation. Whatever, it was just another nail in the coffin of the poor old Murray River. The general public have no idea of the sizes of these modern pumps, and the amount they suck out, particularly for large corporate enterprises.

It seemed we were only just back to sleep when we ran into a very large snag. It required some action, so I jumped out of my swag and into the tinny, while Matt grabbed the long handled shovel and started pushing off the snag. Just as the outboard roared into life, a light was suddenly switched on the southern bank, "Who are you?" an anxious voice yelled out. "We're just drifting through the night," I yelled as we extricated the raft with several curses. They wouldn't have been able to see a thing, just the noise and curses, and they weren't game to put a torch on us. As we drifted off, I yelled "Getting any fish?" and Matt yelled, "What's for breakfast?"

"Sausages," they replied, then silence. Matt reckoned they probably thought we were fishing inspectors, and had nets in but you don't see too many public servants working at 2a.m unless they're on night shift. Anyway, it will give them food for thought, no matter what they were having for breakfast.

A lazy day was followed by a relatively uneventful second night. Around midday the following day we rounded a bend and there was a very large vessel tied up on the Victorian side. It was the "Last Resort", and belonged to some friends of mine, Paul and Ziggy Abend who have been living on the river for the past 21 years. The "Last Resort" is an impressive craft built of steel 20 metres long and weighing 40 tonnes, and very comfortably furnished. They were as surprised to see me as I was them, and invited us on board for lunch. They were tied up at a friend's property and they said I was welcome to leave the raft there. A bit earlier than we had planned, but it was a good situation, so we tied up, unloaded and did the vehicle transfers. The Magic Carpet is an ongoing story.

7

Crossing Lake Torrens

Lake Torrens has a claim to fame. It is the world's longest salt lake located on the western side of the Flinders Ranges; it runs north south for around 200kms, with an area of some 5,800 sq km.

It is located in semi desert station country. The eastern side mostly sand hills and sand plain, while the western side comprises Gibber Plain "tableland". No doubt because of this geology it is a lot deeper on the western side.

Like Lake Eyre to the north it had never actually filled (literally) in white man's memory (Lake Eyre did in 1974) although there are vague reports of it being filled in the early days, just before South Australia was settled.

In 1989, the Flinders Ranges received its greatest rainfall in European memory, most of the western catchment pouring down the west flowing gum creeks into the lake. It filled in a fairly short period.

I had a camel camp located well above one of these tributaries on Mernamora Station, and the water ran under the caravan located there. So I was sort of aware of what was happening.

As that rain was falling I wondered about the possibility of a boat expedition on Lake Torrens, and soon decided on it.

I quickly arranged a party comprising of Sue Keon-Cohen, an old mate and retired judge; Harry Emery; plus a reporter from "The Advertiser" called Brunette Lenkic. Bill Oliver was driving the second boat, and Fred Osmond with his offsider Bots was my back-up driver, to pick us up at the end of the trip – wherever that happened to be.

In June we drove up to the southern end of the lake near Beda Hill, an impressive landmark near the south western corner. It was a very attractive location with some red sand dunes and vegetation consisting of native pine, mulga and black oak etc. The elevated ground gave good views across the lake, with the Flinders dominating the eastern horizon. To the north, the lake ran to the horizon. The western side comprised of the higher ground of the Gibbler Tableland. We were travelling in my old Toyota troop carrier with boats on a trailer and the roof rack.

Channel Nine was very interested in filming this expedition, and was going to arrive in a day or two to file a story.

After an idyllic camp, we finished loading the boats and pushed off. Fred and Bots poured their second cup of coffee, looking forward to spending two or three days at the camp, before heading north toward our pick-up sight.

The conditions were perfect with the sun sitting above the Flinders, promising the usual good weather for this part of the world.

My route was up the west coast, keeping around three or four kilometres off shore, as midday approached the lake and sky on the northern horizon became one, as it does on Lake Eyre. Mirages played their usual tricks, particularly stumps or dead timber on the lake shores, often appearing way larger than they were.

Most of the time Bill would travel parallel with me 50-100 metres away, or would sometimes drop back in my wake. For the most part, people "veged" out, often dozing in the sun. Being June, I didn't have canvas canopies fitted to the boats.

We headed into a little peninsula and boiled the billy for lunch under a needle-wood tree.

After lunch we resumed our northern course. Much of the next few days the Flinders Ranges entertained us with an ever-changing kaleidoscope of colours. From our low position in the boat the land between the lake and ranges could not be seen, and the water of the lake appeared to run right up to the base of the ranges. If I didn't know different, I could be tempted to alter course, and motor right up into Brachina Gorge, or across to the Parachilna Pub for a beer!

About mid afternoon, the Channel Nine chopper disturbed the peace in a dramatic fashion. It circled us low several times, the cameraman filming us out of the open doorway, before travelling north for more filming.

That afternoon I made camp on shore, picking a location that had some dead timber. An hour later the chopper returned, landing near the camp. The crew spent the night with us, doing some interviews. It filmed us departing the next morning before taking off for Adelaide, leaving us to our peaceful existence.

It was Sue's 48th birthday that day, and I thought about making something special for dinner that evening. We looked at a couple of shore locations, and about mid afternoon were cruising along about 200m off shore, when we saw a lone emu skulking along not far from the lake shore. Then a head and neck appeared out of the low bush like a periscope, and another emu sprang up, both of them running off. We went into shore, keeping our eyes on the spot where the emus had jumped up. Landing, we walked over to the spot and sure enough there was a nest with seven eggs in it. The fact that they didn't rattle, and the low number probably indicated that the female was still laying. I took one reassuring the girls that it would soon be replaced as we headed off in the boats; the two emus were making their way back to the nest. When the female finished laying, she would shoot through leaving the male to incubate and bring up the chicks. Emus knew all about women's liberation before Germaine Greer came on the scene.

It was about two hours to dark, and I had the option of camping on shore, or making for the first of the small islands. We were about to pass the large west flowing gulf called the Carrapateena Lake. We decided on the island option and opened up the outboards to full throttle. As it neared sundown, the colours were absolutely breath-taking; the water was like silk without a breath of wind to mar its surface. The brilliant sunset colours of red, gold and colours in between reflected back across the water toward the Flinders Ranges that formed a beautiful pinkish back drop.

The sun disappeared and the temperature dropped with it, as we bored on toward the un-named island, a small smudge on the horizon, a light breeze appeared from the sou-west, not adding to our comfort. It produced six inch waves, but didn't slow us down to any degree. I looked back and noticed Harry sitting up the front of Bill's boat. He was hunched up in the cold, and reminded me a bit of a night heron, the way they seem to hump their shoulders.

Finally, the island loomed up in the darkness and we were all very relieved to arrive. It wouldn't have been hard to miss it, as there was no moon.

We landed on a nice little beach with some needlewoods and other shrubbery. As soon as the motors were off, we could hear the loud calls of nesting birds, although none were in evidence. Sue's birthday dinner consisted of what I call an emu "conglomerate" a sort of mix between an omelette and scrambled egg. A very tasty dish, and one, always looked forward to.

A very good camp and a birthday I think she will always remember. Next morning we surveyed our surroundings. It was just a small island of a few acres. No stilts nesting, but a number of plover and black fronted dotterels. There were a lot of silver gull and terns on the far side of the island, being responsible for most of the noise.

We headed off into another perfect day seeing the very large Andamooka Island to the west. I would like to have checked that out in detail, but time didn't permit.

Later we arrived at Murdie Island with the almost deafening cries of thousands of pied stilts, whose breeding that year was causing much excitement amongst

Rex Ellis

A golden morning on the Murray River

Boat camp on Lake Eyre Island

The Warburton River

Camp on Warburton River

Boating into Birdsville

Camp on Cooper Creek

Cooper Creek in flood

Author about to embark on failed attempt to cross Lake Eyre

Diamantina River

Dingo crossing Warburton River

Dingo

Low water Kallakoopah Creek expedition Simpson desert S.A.

Lunch camp
Diamantina
Creek

Lunch camp
Warburton
River

'Magic
Carpet'
Murray River

Young wedgetailed eagles on nest Warburton River

More vegetation than Water Georgina River

Mending Avon inflatable Murray River raft safari

Negotiating headwaters of Mitchell River Cape York Peninsula Qld

Paroo River

Peregrine falcon at nest

Warburton River country in a good year Poached Egg's in foreground

The catching of rabbits that made their way to the camp oven

Kallakoopah Creek Simpson Desert

Warburton River (low water)

Diamantina River Sturt Stony desert (Qld)

Sinking of 'Water Rat' Victoria River N.T.

Starting out on Lake Torrens crossing Flinders Range in background

Diamantina River (Qld)

Sunset on 'Lake Gregory'

Tawny frogmouth

An idyllic boat camp Warburton River

The 'Dog Fence' A man made barrier on Paroo-River (Qld - NSW Border)

Warburton Cliffs natural erosion patterns

Warburton River Cliffs

Pelicans Warburton River

A misty morning

Warburton River

White bellied sea eagle

Approaching mouth of Lake Eyre Warburton River

Dawn on Cooper Creek

The Author and 'Stubby' Lake Eyre "Badlands"

Preparing Lunch, Cooper Creek
Georgina Ellis & Stony

ornithologists. There were some red necked avocets, but difficult to say if they were nesting. Seagulls have bred to un-natural populations since European settlement, and are one of the biggest threats to the future of pied stilts predating on their eggs and chicks. However, on this occasion there was no evidence of this. We photographed nests, but didn't walk around too much, not wanting to disturb this very important event.

North of here there were other smaller un-named islands that also had large concentrations of stilts, but we didn't disturb them. There was another small island further to the north where they hadn't been reported, and I thought I would check it out. Well before we reached it, there were clouds of stilts evident, and we pulled up to boil the billy. There were many nesting stilts there as well, and it put a bit of a dampener on the lunch time conversation! This island lay off the tip of Andamooka Island. We thought 15,000-20,000 birds, but it was hard to estimate. Here there were gulls hanging around the edges of the colony, many were standing right next to the nesting stilts, and it was obvious they had evil intentions.

In 2000, when Lake Eyre held a lot of water, the silver gulls almost decimated the colonies of breeding stilts. A lot of pressure was put on the National Parks and Wildlife Service, who eventually conducted a bread poisoning operation by helicopter, aimed at the silver gulls. This reduced the numbers to the extent that the stilts bred a second time with successful hatchings.

Our camp that night was on the northern end of the Andamooka Island.

Next day we proceeded on up the lake, occasionally striking shallow water, travel was only half that of the following day. Camped once again on the western shore. We had travelled around 160kms of the 200km long lake. Most large salt lakes in South Australia become shallow on their northern ends. It was most unlikely that we would be able to travel the full distance, but I wanted to go as far as was possible. I contacted Fred on the radio that night at Arcoona Station, near Woomera, and suggested he move to a point on the lake opposite, and about three quarters of the way up Andamooka Island. There was a little track in there from Bosworth Station.

Next day we headed off once again, and ran into shallow water almost straight away. Up until lunch (which we ate in the boats) it was more out than in the boats, pushing and pulling them through water about a foot deep. We made another eight kilometres, but I could see we had done our dash. The water would not get any deeper, and a slight wind change from the north or north west, even though unlikely at this time of the year, could see us stranded on the mud. The mirages were tantalising us to the north, throwing up shimmering distorted images of sand hills and trees, but it simply wasn't on.

We turned the boats around, and for the first time in five days, headed south. I had had a radio chat with Fred at lunch time but was unable to contact him on the Little Codan.

About 5p.m. I pulled into shore near some mulga, and tried Fred again. I know he was listening on the hour, but still couldn't get him. We were only about 16kms from our rendezvous, but I didn't want to travel after dark with the party, if he wasn't going to be there.

So I decided I would go down quickly in the Avon inflatable to see if he was at the location. Taking minimal tucker and my swag, I took off just after sundown. With the lightly loaded boat I was able to get up on the plane. I wasn't concerned about hitting anything in the way of snags and the water was at a consistent depth of a metre and a half. There was enough starlight for me to see the silhouette of the land and also Andamooka Island.

I travelled for about half an hour like this, but slowed things down when I ploughed into a big gob of mud and nearly got chucked out of the boat. Soon after I saw the welcome sight of Fred's campfire, and almost put it out when I pulled up at his camp on the lake's edge. Fred and Bots had heard me for the last half hour. They had been listening on their radio, but hadn't heard us. This happens every now and then with radio reception or maybe one of our radios had a problem.

Fred is a grape grower at McLaren Flat and produced one of his "special" bottles of home made reds, and after trying to contact Bill unsuccessfully, we settled down to a feed and yarn, the reds only improving the situation.

Early next morning I put some extra fuel on board, and headed back to the boat camp. Bill was all ready to travel; we headed south once again. I was getting used to this stretch of lake.

About 10a.m. we arrived back at Fred's camp, unloaded the boats and loaded on to the Toyota and trailer. We drove steadily along the rough wheel track over Gibber Plains towards Bosworth homestead. Looking behind us, you wouldn't credit that there was a massive lake full of fresh water a few kilometres away.

After a while the corrugated iron buildings of Bosworth Station came into view surrounded by the rolling Gibber Plains.

Max Greenfield welcomed us, very interested to hear how we had got on. He put the kettle on and invited us to an excellent lunch of cold saltbush mutton, surely one of the greatest meats there is. We knocked up a salad from our leftover veggies. Max was a bachelor and on his own at Bosworth.

After lunch he bought out a bundle, opening it up on the verandah it was a rug made entirely from rabbit skins. Only the best fur along the top of the backs had been used, and around 80 rabbits made the contribution. He said that an aunty of his had made it years ago.

Saying our goodbyes, we headed for Woomera and south, having completed a journey that may not be possible again in our lifetime.

8

Roper River

In September 2003, my son-in-law Nick Brooks and I arrived at Roper Bar. With us were Don Ziino and Phil Cuffley, "guinea pigs" for this first trip down the Roper. After a visit to the Roper Bar Store, we made our way to their boat ramp, a very steep one about three kilometres away. We launched the Water Rat, and I took the Oka back to a lock up compound at the store, getting a lift back to the river.

We got going about 11a.m. but soon discovered that one of our batteries seemed a bit dicey, so after boiling the billy and having lunch, we returned a kilometre or so to the ramp and tied up. I phoned the store on my sat phone and eventually a new battery was delivered. We set off once again down the Roper. A different river to the Victoria.

From Roper Bar it is navigable for some 120 kilometres to the Gulf of Carpentaria. It forms the southern boundary of Arnhem Land on the north bank, and cattle stations to the south. There is a much smaller variation in tides compared to the Victoria, but you still need to keep your wits about you. The vegetation is thicker on the banks with some rain forest species being present.

We had a couple of opera house traps baited with soap for red claw a delectable fresh water crayfish and good barramundi bait. The trouble is they are so tasty they don't always make it onto the hooks for the barra!

Finding suitable camps on these rivers is always a challenge, because the first priority is getting up away from the crocs. That often means carting all your camp gear up a steep bank, and on the Roper, through a tangle of bush. But mostly we succeeded in getting camps with a good view over the river, often through a screen of bush. Nick, a very keen fisherman, would head off in the Avon inflatable after a barra, and provided a few on this trip, as well as a number of catfish, under-rated but good eating.

Spent the next three days getting down to the mouth. The fresh water cuts out around about half way down, and the river widens by half a kilometre in some places. Only signs of habitation are the Ngukurr Aboriginal settlement on the Arnhem Land side. There were several islands and the boiler of an early wreck of the paddle steamer Young Australian.

There were also several tributaries but decided to explore them on the next trip. We camped one night on the end of Kangaroo Island, the largest on the river. It took an hour or so to do the last couple of kilometres due to a heavy wind blowing against the incoming tide, causing waves half a metre high. On these occasions I attach canvas to the front and sides of the Water Rat, giving me more free board. Works really well.

We had a sheltered camp in the bush, right on the end of a small point. Once the tide was in, the bank was only a metre and a half above the water, but we had a good fire and plenty of wood to keep any crocs away.

Due to the mosquitoes and sandflies at the time of year on the coast, we were using a big mosquito dome to camp in, and every night put on a liberal dose of our special sandfly brew each evening.

In the morning we had a pea souper fog, with visibility down to about 50 metres, but it cleared before we left.

We had smoko on Hawk's Nest Island, a little rocky island of about half an acre with an old white bellied sea eagle's nest in a tree.

Nick caught a 10 pound barra later on when we were tied up for lunch. Good size for eating.

We had our first mangrove camp, easy for access – plenty of grassy flats with belts of mangroves, only problem (apart from the increased mozzies and sandflies) the banks were low. We collected a big wood heap and slept close to the fire, stoking it through the night, rifle always handy just in case. Don and Phil had a bad night with the sandflies here. Don in particular was suffering with a lot of sandfly bites. Some people have this problem, no matter how much they look after themselves. Not a complaint from Don as is normal, but I was feeling for him. A white tailed nightjar gave its distinctive call all night, and we had seen it earlier hawking for insects around the fire.

Nearer to the coast we passed a failed prawn farm operation. Near here we went a couple of kilometres up one of the tributaries – narrow water ways (five to eight metres wide) meandering into Arnhem Land with thick mangroves either side. Did some fishing here, but nothing. Nick went off in the dinghy at lunch time for a fish, and saw a large snake in the water.

That night a decent camp was hard to find, so we anchored in the river and camped for the night. This involved placing three large marine ply boards across the bench seats and juggling gear around a bit. Nick camped up on the top and the three of us on the bottom. We cooked our meal on a gas stove, however, after an hour or two, the mozzies and sandflies proved too much that I pulled up anchor and moved to the middle of the river. A nice breeze out there, and most (some) of us had a good night. Toilet arrangements were interesting, involving use of the fire bucket on top of the boat.

Half an hour's travel next morning bought us to Paul's fishing camp. Very good bloke, offering us his place to camp if we wanted it. A little further on we called into a large Vietnamese fishing camp (crabbers). Half a dozen huts on stilts above the river. Very hospitable, they gave us a pack of mosquito coils that they swear by; we swapped them for two tins of vanilla rice cream. Another 10 kilometres bought us to the mouth of the Roper, which was around two kilometres wide.

I was keen to head up the coast north to a creek some 10 kilometres distant; however, the wind was blowing making it too rough to be safe. We tied up for a few hours and caught some good size catfish, then camped up a small creek on a mangrove flat and everyone (I think) had a good night's sleep.

Really heavy dew next morning and cool weather, the tide was out, and after breakfast tried following a channel to get us out in the gulf. Kept running aground and made worse by the tilt on my outboard going on the blink. Eventually got out into the gulf, and when we were in only a couple of feet of water, we hopped out and pulled the tilt off, but couldn't fix it. Continued on through water one to one and half metres deep if we kept to a narrow channel. Eventually arrived at Painnyilatya Creek, camping half a kilometre up from the mouth. We had the afternoon here. Turned out to be a good camp, we went four kilometres up the creek in the inflatable until it became too narrow. Also had a good walk along the back of the beach, and Phil found a very good piece of green cargo netting washed up in a low mangrove. We took it back to camp and Nick rigged up an excellent hammock inside the boat that is still in use today. It's so popular that people have to book a session in it.

Caught a feed of catfish, and an excellent meal was had washed down with a nice cold Penfold's Chardonnay.

In the morning I got up for a leak and first thing I noticed was a 10 foot salty lying on top of the water under our anchor rope. I showed the others and he very soon sunk out of sight. Left at 8a.m. and just caught the first tide to get out of the creek mouth. Some shallow water, then up to two metres all the way back to the mouth.

Back up the Roper to the Vietnamese camp and lunch with "Lanny" in his hut. This involved me asking him to lunch –our lunch, his venue. He gave us some dried fish, which was very tasty, the way they do it. Called into Paul's camp again then motored another 12 kilometres up the river to a mangrove camp on the Arnhem

Land side. Plenty of agile wallabies here. I cooked a "sausage wok up" and Nick made a very nice cherry duff.

Saw about 30 crocs that day at low tide on the mud banks, the largest about 13 feet. Later that afternoon I just happened to catch a glimpse of an opening in the dense mangroves, went back for a look and discovered a very interesting camp. Someone had done a lot of work paving a walking track some 30 metres with flat stones to a camp at the back of the mangroves on a big open plain. A couple of old timber and iron huts and wrecks of two vehicles. We camped a couple of kilometres further up river on another open plain. This would be the last mozzie/sandfly camp – as soon as you're out of the mangroves they are not a problem.

Next day we pulled in opposite a fair lump of a hill called Mount Roper and tied up. The weather was into the 40's, but we had made the decision earlier to climb it. We headed off about 10a.m. walking across a big grassy plain. The range was about three kilometres away. Half a kilometre from the foot of the range we came across a lagoon with a bit of birdlife on it. At the base of the range we came into lancewood timber. It's the acacia that replaces mulga in the tropics. Quite straight and possibly harder. Nick and I cut four big logs on the way south, and we duly made a door for my office. A delightful timber looking very much like mulga.

It took us about 40 minutes to get to the top, but couldn't enjoy the view because of a good cover of eucalypts on top. Walked half a kilometre along the top of the range and up a bit higher to the top of a large trig. A very good view was to be had of the area, the Roper snaking off toward the coast, and could just see the water of the gulf in the heat haze. After 20 minutes or so we made our way back along the top of the range. We climbed down a bit checking out some overhangs, but nothing of interest. Very hot walking back across the plain and eventually arrived back at the boat at 2p.m. for a late lunch.

No matter how hot it is on shore and away from the river, it is always beautifully cool on the boat under the canopy, usually a breeze of some kind on the river.

The next couple of days were spent heading leisurely back upstream, fishing and birding.

Arriving back at the landing, I set out to walk the three and half kilometres to the Roper River Store because they forgot to deliver the Oka, very hot. Half way along the track a Toyota pulled up and I met the previous owner of Urapunga Station (now the Arnhem Land Aboriginal settlement) a man called Ray Fryer. Good bloke and gave me some iced water. I picked up the Oka, returned to the landing and loaded the boat. Nick took the Avon and went the four kilometres or so up to the landing at the caravan park where we met him.

ROPER RIVER, SECOND TRIP

We had a day off (in theory) mostly spent cleaning boat up etc. Next afternoon my next crew was bought in by road from Mataranka. They were Dennis and Kath Dyason (old clients of mine) and Marie de Monchaux; Trevor Shiell had arrived earlier from Alice Springs with Bill Oliver on board his Troopie. Bill was offsiding this trip. Trevor headed down to the coast and arrived back that evening with a nice feed of barramundi for the evening meal.

A good evening was spent and a fine feed. Next morning Trevor headed back to Alice with Don, Phil and Nick while we finished provisioning the Water Rat and putting it back in the river.

We headed off about 11a.m., very slow over a lot of rock close to the surface until we got to the mouth of the Wilton River. We headed up it three kilometres and had lunch, with a nice white bellied sea eagle entertaining us. Back down to the Roper and on down stream to the Hodgskins River. About 25 metres wide with gallery rain forest both sides. We went up three kilometres and found a good camp on high banks, fished but with no luck.

Next morning a bit further up the river we came across a large flying fox colony. The air was thick with them, the trees covered and the smell intense. Lying on the surface was a 10 foot croc, possibly waiting for young fruit bats to fall in the water. Good photography, these colonies are always interesting.

We headed back to the Roper, camping further down. Bill caught a nice spotted grunter and we got four nice cherapins in the net using soap. Supposed to be for bait but they are so tasty we had them for hors doeuvres. Bill and I are both slept on top of the Water Rat, anchored out, and it worked well.

We passed Green Island next day and that afternoon found a good camp at the foot of a Lancewood Hill, flat level ground with a tunnel like track through some lignum to get to it. Weather is hot and it's noticed when you come ashore. Can't swim of course, so we have a shower session every evening with a bucket on the foredeck. We were fishing that afternoon and followed a whipsnake across the river. Less than a metre long with a white head and yellow body.

Next day I took a good long lens shot of a jabiru with a mud crab in its bill, which would have kept him busy. Then a beautiful maroon and white brahminy kite swooped down and tried to steal it, but I missed that on film.

We arrived at the fishing camp about 4p.m. and met Merle Reed; she was the fisherman's mother-in-law. Lived at Adelaide River but spent a fair bit of time here. She made us very welcome and invited us to stay in some hut and caravan accommodation because of the sandflies being bad. We were happy to accept. Bill and I camped outside in our swags. We ate the jew fish that Dennis had caught and it was very tasty. A good fun night was had by all and I think Merle was glad of the company. When we were unloading our gear from the boat we had 20 metres of deep grey mud to wade through, as tide was low. Demonstrating that chivalry still exists, I was giving Kath a piggy back to shore, half way there I went arse up in the mud, providing a spectacle for all and sundry.

Next day we left our camp and taking Merle with us headed down to the mouth, we went out in the gulf for about three hours fishing and had lunch there, but not a bite was had.

Coming back through the mouth we came in with a following sea of metre high waves, and I put up my canvas sides. We went over to a 130 foot deep hole that Merle knew of and tried our luck – but no luck. We then headed up a mangrove creek where I got a quick glimpse of a great billed heron, which made my day, not a common bird. Bill caught a nice eight pound barramundi. On the way back we called into the Vietnamese fishing camp. Merle said something and they gave us a box of mud crabs, we dropped everyone back at Merle's place and Bill and I returned in the Avon to pull our own crab nets. Three crabs; one big one got loose in the boat and tried to yard me up. I made sure he didn't because they are quite capable of breaking a big toe, formidable claws! That night we had a big crab cleaning/cooking session in an old copper full of boiling water, and a memorable feed was had. Not many better feeds than mud crabs.

Big motoring day the following day headed back to Blackfellow Creek and went up two and half kilometres for a look. Then back to the "Lancewood" camp. Making 66 kilometres for the day. Saw crimson finches that evening. Barramundi for tea, and we slept well.

Plenty of fishing next day, but all catfish. We camped high on a sandy bank having to hack our way through a lot of Parkonsonia and Rubber Vine, two nasty noxious plants out of control in many areas.

The last couple of days we fished and explored other creeks. In one I saw a pacific bazza (crested hawk), a large raptor that does lots of "tumbling". Both in the air, and in trees. Really good, as I hadn't seen one for years.

We finished up back at the caravan park and loaded the boat in 40 degree temperatures. Then headed to Mataranka dropping Dennis, Kath and Maree off at a motel. Bill and I then drove south.

9

Diamantina Voyage – 1999

There were exceptional summer rains in 1999, and the Diamantina was looking like being a big river. I rang up a few of my "regulars" who know the true meaning of the word "adventure" and we were on our way within 10 days. It was February and very hot, and I had Bill Oliver with me in my other boat, and the party consisted of Brenton Hicks, Tony Bomford, Jenny Chapman and Eilleen Nelson. A night camped out on the Birdsville Track and into Birdsville about lunchtime with the temperature around 45 degrees celsius.

I had arranged for some mates, Don and Lynette Rowlands to come up river with us and bring the Oka back to Birdsville. I planned on travelling right down to Goyders Lagoon Swamp and then back up river to Pandi Pandi Station.

We drove out past the Bluff (Roseberth Station) and pulled up at Stony Crossing Waterhole, a bit downstream from Durri Station where it breaks into a lot of channel country.

We spent a good night camped on the waterhole, with Lynette catching half a dozen black bream. She has always been a very good fisherman (woman).

It didn't take long to load up, and on this trip Brenton had his canoe with him, being very keen in that area. He has done a lot of very physical trips over the years, including some big camel expeditions with me. Climbed mountains overseas, and took one of his boys across the Kokoda Track, so I had no worries regarding him and his canoe.

Donald and Lynette headed off in the Oka, and we headed off in the boats. I hadn't been down this section to Birdsville, so I was anticipating it more than usual. It was all through Sturt Stony Desert and cattle country.

There had been good local rains and the country was looking good with a lot of green amongst the red. The downside was that the flies were in their billions, I was even putting fly repellent around Stubbie's eyes.

We had a fairly hairy bit of travel across the Stony Crossing before we were in deep water. I had one of my Stacer punts, and Bill was in the Avon inflatable. He had rigged a very rough looking tarp propped up with a coolibah framework, to keep the sun off him. Brenton was in his red canoe skimming along with the current.

We struck quite a lot of thick coolibah across the river in some sections giving us a bit of strife; particularly Bill with is makeshift canopy.

Lunch saw us camped under a huge coolibah and Stubbie was soon 30 feet up amongst its branches as is his habit.

We were on the lookout for the inland taipan or fierce snake as it is sometimes called. They are the most venomous snake in the world, but fortunately are very shy. Can be easily confused with the king brown snake which has larger scales on its head, and is usually a larger snake. The king brown is not as shy, but to my knowledge there has never been a recorded European death from the bite of a king brown.

The inland taipan is a relatively new discovery, not being recognised until the 1960's. I will mention an incident that occurred just up river from us in the late 1960's. A safari operator who was also a snake expert was operating out of the Gosford Reptile Park in NSW, owned by the late Eric Worrell. (Eric had been on a number of my trips collecting reptiles in long sleeved shirts, that he used to book back through the airlines as general cargo – that might test out the current airline security. Nowadays I would probably have to dob him in as a suspicious person!).

This particular operator would collect a number of snakes on his trips, taking them back to the Gosford Reptile Park. On this occasion he went to catch what he thought was a king brown snake, which wasn't too much of a problem for an experienced snake catcher.

He was bitten by this snake, and very quickly exhibited symptoms that were not unlike a king brown bite. Fortunately he was close to Durri Station, and the Flying Doctor was called from Charleville. He was flown straight to the Queen Elizabeth Hospital in Adelaide, where my sister Dianne, was a theatre nurse at the time. His condition was very serious and his wife was flown over. Dianne was looking after him, and apparently he was lucky to live. It turned out that he had been bitten by an inland taipan.

Although he lived, the bite took its toll and he had to give the safari work away.

On the third morning we were approaching the bluff on Roseberth Station homestead, and unbeknown to us, Jeff Morton, the owner, was working on a windmill on the river near the homestead. We rounded the bend and saw him staring at us with a bit more than usual interest. We pulled up and he told us how he could hear this engine noise that he couldn't work out. He knew it was none of his vehicles, or an aircraft, and anyway it didn't sound like a vehicle. The last thing he thought of was boats!

He invited us up for smoko, and we spent a pleasant hour with Jeff and Bev Morton. The homestead and buildings are situated on a big bluff above the Diamantina, having probably the best view of any station on the river. The waterhole below and then floodplain and channel country stretching to the red sand dune on the far horizon. To the south were the Gibber Plains of Sturt Stony Desert.

Off down river again, camping about six kilometres upstream from Birdsville.

In the morning we approached the Birdsville Bridge, which was completely covered with water. I reckoned we would be able to pass over it with our outboards raised, and proceeded to do so. Next minute there was a loud bang that half threw us out of our seats. I had hit the steel top of one of the bridge uprights that had a piece of vegetation wrapped around it, which is why I hadn't seen it. We pulled into the shore, and I found there was a dent as big as a fist near the keel where it enters the water. If it had been anything else other than one of these heavy duty Stacers, it probably would have put a hole in the boat.

We had the interesting experience of motoring right into Birdsville, pulling up at the caravan park. We had a counter lunch at the pub. Before returning to the boats. Nell and Deline Brook came down and saw us off. On our way back across the floodplain to the river, we took a couple of "funny fotos" pulling my boat up to a "Please drop bull dust here" sign, which just had the top of the sign sticking out above the floodwater. Bull dust was a bit scarce at the moment.

On down the river again, through more familiar territory, although I had only been down to the swamp once before.

We reckoned we were over the Queensland border, although there was no sign of it on the river. Soon after we had the delightful sight of a dozen red tailed black cockatoos sweeping over us with their plaintive call and flying low along the water in front. They landed in a large coolibah where some more birds were sitting. This is an isolated small colony and the same sub species as is found around Alice Springs. It is thought that they probably crossed the Simpson Desert from the Hale River (where they are resident) in an exceptionally good season, but who knows? David Morton from Pandi Pandi Station said he has always been aware of them in the area. They stick to that part of the river from the border, down to Goyders Lagoon swamp. I have never seen or heard of them around Birdsville.

Don Rowlands had left my Oka at Pandi, so we called in there next morning and had smoko with David and Jane Morton.

The weather was hot, which meant plenty of time swimming and the heat really wasn't a problem. The flies were though. I don't think I have ever struck them so bad. It was impossible to take a mouthful of food without swallowing a dozen or so. I told people that you have to just look upon them as "protein", this is the healthiest country in the world, its extreme aridity guarantees that the flies aren't going to make you crook, just send you mad! If you let them. If we put a piece of meat on a plate, in a second it was literally black with flies. Some of the party were wearing fly nets, but I reckon they are more irritating than the flies.

I did have a flyscreen dome, and we started having our meals in there like a mob of arid eskimos. That kept the flies to a minimum.

Just after dusk the flies would knock off, and there would be a pause of about 10 minutes before the mosquitoes took over. They were bad enough, causing us to retire to our swags and nets earlier than normal. Sand flies were around, but not as bad as they can be.

Most of my summer boat trips are not too badly affected by flies and mozzies (nothing a good repellent can't handle) but this trip was certainly an exception. One night when the flies were particularly bad, Bill really 'spat the dummy'. He was preparing the last of our fresh meat (steaks) for cooking, placing them on our little wooden table. I heard #*!!!**#=!! And saw Bill stalking off into the bush. His body language indicating he wasn't happy. I walked over to the camp and Brenton was holding some unidentifiable objects in his hands, helpless with mirth. It was our meal totally covered in a myriad of bush flies! Anyway, later on even Bill pronounced it was a good meal, so it just goes to show – you have to keep perspective.

We took a nice little narrow channel, weaving our way through large coolibahs for a couple of kilometres to have a look at Lake Coriwillannie I had been here before by vehicle some years ago when there was a bit of water in it. The channel entered the northern end, and it was a good sight stretching south to the horizon. We camped half way up a sand dune overlooking the lake, and had a good walk around, finding plenty of Aboriginal artefacts, mainly grinding and hammer stones.

Back again next morning and on down the river. The usual plentiful birdlife, but nothing out of the ordinary. Saw a pair of spotted harriers at the lake. About 12 dingoes so far this trip. Called into the old Clifton Hills ruins and they hadn't changed much since 1982 when I was there last.

Reached Goyders Lagoon Swamp about 4p.m. and headed along the eastern edge for about three kilometres on a nice narrow deep channel. Made our camp here, a good one, but under nets soon after dark as the mosquitoes were in droves.

Spent all next morning exploring the swamp as much as possible. We would keep going in on channels until they became too narrow, shallow or disappeared. Had to be careful not to get lost in this maze of waterways. It was interesting though – a sea of water and huge lignum bushes. We had lunch under a coolibah at the base of a sand dune on the north east corner of the swamp, before beginning our trip back to Pandi. It was against the current, so most of the time we towed Brenton's canoe. A pleasant but uneventful few days saw us at Pandi, where we loaded up and headed off down the Birdsville Track.

It looked like the flood might get through to the Warburton and down to Lake Eyre, and I had plans ready if it did.

10

Warburton River Journeys – 1999, 2000, 2001 & 2004

During these years, enough rain fell particularly in the inland of Queensland, accompanied by good tropical monsoons, to keep the Warburton running almost non-stop into Lake Eyre.

In this period I operated 10 Warburton River boat safaris plus the Kallakoopah expedition.

Of all the desert rivers I have been fortunate enough to travel down, the Warburton is my favourite. The scenery is ever changing and sometimes very spectacular. We normally begin from several locations near Kalamurina Station, depending on the flood levels. During those years Trevor Edwards the Kalamurina manager would always give me up to date information on the river when I rang him prior to a trip. He knows that country like the back of his hand.

A lot of trips, we would leave from a crossing on a creek, a couple of kilometres from the river, giving a pleasant little cruise through submerged vegetation before breaking out into the main river. There is always high excitement in the party because these trips are right up with the greatest outback adventures available. There is an element of risk and danger, ingredients any true adventure must have. I am very well aware of the risks and am well prepared for them. My main concern is a bad breakdown or being stranded, something that could cost me an awful lot of money.

The desert camel trekking that we do is another unique Australian experience, but is far more labour intensive than running the boat safaris. Like the camel expeditions we never or rarely see another person.

When we get into the river from this creek, it is about 80 to 100 metres wide, with scattered coolibah and coobah along its banks. Very soon we come to Stony Crossing where we tore the bottom out of an inflatable in 1982. Here we take it very carefully, even with the Stacers, sometimes the river is a bit lower with little depth over the crossing, and we then have to start our trip just downstream from the crossing. There is around half a days travel to the first of the "cliffs". I have my own names for all of the cliffs and any other significant landmarks like large sand dunes or unusual shaped trees. Of the three days I normally take to do the 140 kilometres to Lake Eyre, a bit over a day is travelling past intermittent cliffs. Some are only 60 metres or so long, with others extending for several kilometres. They are all different. Probably the most spectacular are the naturally eroded cliffs of hard off white sand and white clay. As they back drop toward the river with different levels there are thousands of vertical "spires" of sand or clay from several inches to several metres in height, looking like giant curry combs. In the morning and afternoon when shadows are present the effects are spectacular indeed, and of great photographic interest.

Others are sheerer and honey coloured. Those and their early or late reflections in the river is a real eyeful.

Another small cliff called the "Ploughshare" is a real favourite for photography in the mornings. One of the longest I call "Redcliff", as it is comprised of red dirt and huge gypsum crystals (up to a metre of more high). The top few metres are of a darker colour providing contrast and they are about 20 metres high.

There is another spot in the big cliff line I call "Safe Harbour". A narrow little channel winds its way some half a kilometre into a "harbour" of about a quarter acre, and is totally landlocked. We once spent a night camped in here during a howling gale, and a cosy little camp it was. Unfortunately I can only use this on higher rivers as the water dries up quicker than a lot of areas.

On some of the bottom end cliffs there are intriguing little channels meandering inland and always worth the side trip.

Usually the cliffs mean shallow water, and on some of them we have lots of strife with a falling river, particularly heading back up stream. Because our propellers are often churning mud and gravel, we sometimes return with a prop worn down to half the diameter of the original. It says a lot for the work these outboard motors do.

The last little cliff houses that I call "Fairy Martin City", it is the biggest grouping of fairy martin nests (bottle shaped of mud) I have ever seen. I estimate there are around 200 of them on an overhang a few metres above an average river.

When the cliffs finish the timber seems especially thick and lush. In a good season it is a wonderful haven for bird life, with at times, marvellous shows of wild flowers. Commonest being poached egg (scenecio), yellowtop and wild parsnip.

Eventually the timber begins to thin out, as you approach what I call the "Long Broadwater"; this is where the river widens up to half a kilometre with scattered timber along the banks. The Simpson Desert to the north and the Tirari Desert to the south are now much more evident from the boats, especially on a higher river.

At the end of the "Long Broadwater" the river suddenly turns to the north, becoming a narrow fast running channel of about 10 to 15 metres in width. All the trees disappear except for a few dead coolibahs. Some young coolibah and some stunted coobah and smaller acacias along the edge of the channel.

This is an exciting area, I call "The Wetlands" and we travel something like six or seven kilometres through here. It is ever changing and one of my more worrying areas, although I have more or less come to terms with it now. On one trip I made the decision to turn around here without visiting the lake (much to the party's disappointment), because I was scared of a stranding. You can only push a heavily laden boat so far without water.

The water in many places is only a matter of inches from the top of the bank, and if it went over the top, navigation would be a nightmare. It did so in 1974, but was so far over that it didn't matter. The birdlife is usually prolific here, and is mostly where you start seeing the big concentrations of pelicans.

You suddenly come out of "The Wetlands", passing the narrow mouth of the Kallakoopah Creek into the Kallakoopah flood out, a body of water up to a kilometre wide. This is where you can come "unstuck" on the return trip finding the narrow channel back into "The Wetlands" quite easily heading up the broad Kallakoopah entrance or the other way out on to boggy flats that run out. The other problem is the shallow water and shifting sandbars of the Kallakoopah floodout, I am always very glad to get back up river from here.

After about four kilometres the floodout runs into the "Lake Eyre Broadwater" or as some maps erroneously call the "Warburton Groove". This is a huge body of water up to a kilometre wide, running through complete desolation for about 10 kilometres to the Warburton mouth and Lake Eyre.

This chapter deals with a few highlights that occurred on the various river safaris from 1999 to 2001. They were mostly 10 day trips, ex-Adelaide or from my place on the Murray River near Morgan. We would get away by about 5.30a.m., driving through to Mungerannie half way up the Birdsville Track. Mungerannie is a cattle station but it's also a very special little bush pub operated by John and Genevieve Hammond. We would often have dinner there; pick up my boat trailer and two boats loaded up with a lot of boat fuel and head off. Sometimes we would camp on the way out to the river, on other occasions we would drive right out to our starting point, and camp there. Mungerannie is always a very welcome stop and I get nothing but hospitality, help and co-operation from John and Genevieve. Either way, it was a long day, but the Oka makes an art form out of making a long day's travel a comfortable relaxing experience.

We would then spend seven days doing the boat trip – three days down to Lake Eyre and four days back against the current.

When the river dropped significantly, Trevor would deliver the Oka sometimes as much as 100 kilometres down the river. This meant we would have more time to spend down the Lake Eyre end. With a high river I would have to come all the way back in the boats, as flood outs and channels made access down river impracticable.

After the first floodwater (the head of the flood) goes through, particularly if it's a big flood, the landscape is often altered quite dramatically. One such occasion was during this period, when a second flood had gone down. We were along soon after and when I approached this spot about half way down the river. I came across a freshly cut channel on the Tirari Desert side, it was very deep, the banks on either side about 10 metres high, and the channel about the same width, and running very fast.

I turned into it, making sure everyone was at "action stations" and life jackets on. We had an exciting ride through there, and could see the banks were going to take a while to "heal up". Big coolibahs and coobahs were hanging down by their roots, while others balanced precariously on the edge of the bank, not having a long future to look forward to. We had to dodge a lot of obstacles and in one place cut through the branches of an upturned coolibah that had fallen into the river.

We travelled about a kilometre before we re-appeared on the other channel, which will now become an anabranch by the look of the lesser flow there. Very exciting to see a new feature of Australia freshly created. A channel plus a large island.

Regarding this particular island, a couple of trips later we had a two night base camp there, and thoroughly explored it. Turned out it had a lot of Aboriginal significance, as we found a couple of big campsites with many old middens and stone artefacts. There was a waterhole nearby that could have been deeper than most, making it a campsite that could last long after the river had ceased to flow.

On one of the high river floods, Stubbie had a bit of drama. We were travelling along and he was standing up in the bow taking great interest in a grey teal doing her broken wing act. A number of species will do this to lead would be predators away from their young. Stubbie did a very uncharacteristic thing. He suddenly jumped into the water to chase the duck. I could see that he was going to be swept into a big lignum swamp, and I could easily lose him in there. I reckoned I had one chance at grabbing him before he went in, so swung the punt around under full power, and bore down on him. I hung over the side to try and grab him by the collar. I touched him but he slipped out of my grasp. The boat ended up being swept unceremoniously into a coolibah. One of the women up the front spotted him and while my wife Patti looked after the motor, I jumped forward and hung over the front and the poor little bugger was clinging tenuously to a thin coolibah branch with his front feet curled around it.

He was about two metres from the boat. I could have jumped in but it was July and the water freezing, however, I had my boots off prepared to on the hope of getting to him before he disappeared into the swamp. I called him and coaxed him and he didn't want to let go of that twig. Finally, he did, and began swimming towards me, his little legs going like eggbeaters. With the current, he was barely making progress and I didn't know how long his strength would last. I hung out as far as possible with the crew hanging on to my legs. He was gradually making ground, and I stretched myself even further with an arm out wishing I hadn't recently cut my fingernails. After what seemed an eternity I finally got my fingers around his collar and dragged a soggy dog on board. He was really knocked up and I reckon that really taught him a lesson. It might have where ducks were concerned, but apparently not with young dingoes.

The following year we came around a bend in the river to find three dingo pups about nine months old playing on a big gob of mud, just metres from the shore. It was too much for Stubbie and he jumped off the front, swimming for the island. The pups ran through shallow water to the shore, disappearing into some lignum. Stubbie followed them and so did I, when I hurriedly pulled the boat in. I pushed through some lignum and a funny sight met my eyes. There was a little clearing in the lignum of about half an acre. Stubbie was playfully chasing one pup and the two others were chasing him! They went round and round in a circle all having the time of their lives. What you see when you haven't got a video. The pups finally took off and Stubbie returned to me.

We were only just underway in the boats, when a fine healthy looking black dingo jumped into the river 50 metres in front of the boats and swam across to the other side. Out of the water, it shook itself and trotted off over the bank without a backward glance.

On the first trip down in 1999 I took an extra large load of fuel, and made fuel dumps at different locations, just in case I needed it on occasion, and indeed I did. You don't like to rely totally on dumped fuel. Over the years I have occasionally had it stolen by low lives in 4WD's, but that isn't a problem on the desert rivers. Some of the hazards here include dingoes chewing the top off, causing evaporation and possibly a dingo addicted to petrol sniffing! They also chew the 120 litre containers, but I currently use very tough, thick polythene ex-pesticide containers, so far a dog hasn't chewed through one. I have gone to use some containers that were not buried after two years, and found them to have evaporated to less than half full, caused by the extreme summer heat, so now I bury them all. On another occasion I left a couple in a gutter in a cliff. When I checked them at a later date, a thunderstorm and quick run off had carried them down the gutter out to the river, where they probably ended up as salt encrusted lumps somewhere out on Lake Eyre.

One trip, I calculated that I would be short of fuel to enable me to go right back to Kalamurina, when I had expected my vehicle to be delivered. Two inches of rain had prevented that, so I organised a pilot I knew to drop me a few jerry cans full of fuel. After a bit of experimenting (providing a good show for us in the boats), it was found that jerry cans (cheap ones) fare a lot better dropped in soft mud, than in the water or on dry land.

Wildlife is always an ongoing "floorshow", particularly the birds. The black whistling kites are constantly above the boats using us as flushing devices. They catch anything from very small water beetles and large insects on the water, to ducklings and other mainly handicapped birds. I have seen a whistling kite with a waterhen in its talons, and a number of times with baby and half grown rabbits. The black kites rely more on carrion, water insects, small reptiles and wounded birds.

The falcons are a thrill to watch particularly the black falcon. This is supposedly the fastest bird in the world in straight flight, and is a thrilling sight when in "overdrive", and pursuing prey. The peregrine is the fastest in a stoop (again supposedly) and will hit a wood swallow or 'bronze wing' pigeon with a "bang". Little falcons are fearless hunters and I have seen one take a teal, a bird larger than itself.

The goshawk and sparrowhawks are the "ram-raiders" of the raptor department, flying straight into a thick tree and plucking some luckless honeyeater off its perch. Brown falcons (Australia's "snake hawk") actually have longer legs with very thick scales to protect them from bites. They also have specially adapted talons for grasping and holding reptiles. Our slowest falcon and most widespread bird of prey with colours ranging from chocolate brown to off white phases, I have seen them pounce on a galah feeding on the ground, and carry it off to a low branch, and many times have seen them catch half grown rabbits.

The two harriers (spotted and swamp) are both seen on the Warbuton, but have only once seen them catch anything – a spotted harrier with a purple swamp hen.

Lots of great experiences with wedgetails, but although we see some on the river, have never seen them catch anything there.

For a long time I was concerned for the welfare of young cormorants and darters. When we went close to their nests hanging over the river in the coolibahs they would often drop like stones from the nest into the water and disappear, so one trip I got the front boat to travel close by their nests causing them to jump out. I drifted along a few minutes late and there they were, climbing back up into their nests; it surely being the biggest adventure they had yet experienced!

I had another surprise with white eye ducks (hardheads). Sometimes you get a lot of young fish floating dead on the river. One theory is that it is caused by certain flood conditions affecting oxygen supply – anyway, it occurs periodically and we saw it during this period. The hardheads were picking up and with some difficulty swallowing these dead fish. I thought I had an ornithological first, until I found out it was a peculiar habit of theirs.

Every trip, the species and concentrations are different. One trip will have white necked (pacific) herons in flocks all down the river, where another trip will see them in their usual single or pair concentrations. Another trip and there were literally hundreds of rufus night herons flying out of about 300 metres of river coobah trees, the most I had seen together anywhere. On two occasions I have woken up in the night to find a night heron standing at the end of my swag, as have others, just curious one supposes. On two different trips I encountered the isolated small population of the large red winged parrot, causing plenty of interest, as there are few parrot species in this area.

Whether you are an ornithologist or not, no-one can help but be impressed by the pelicans. You generally see only a few until you get down closer to the lake. Often we find individuals unable to fly, but still able to fish. They sometimes become "old friends" on consecutive trips, but eventually they disappear, probably falling easy prey to dingoes and wedgetailed eagles.

It's one of nature's great sights to see flocks of many thousands wheeling in the sky above you, riding the thermals. I have my own theory why pelicans take to the thermals in the middle of the day, often disappearing out of sight to the naked eye. Some say they fly for pleasure, but I reckon they fly in order to digest the massive amounts of fish they consume. There's more business than pleasure in the nature world.

You sometimes see pelicans change leaders when flying in the "v" formation, as the bird in front is doing the hard work "breaking the wind" (no pun intended). One of the funniest things I have seen concerning pelicans was a lone pelican attached to the rear of a "v" formation of straw necked ibis. Looked really comical and spoiling the symmetry of the ibis formation.

It is not unusual to hear them fishing at night, accompanied by a sort of paddling noise as they muster up fish. They are not scared to put in the hours, and there are probably not too many union reps amongst them.

Their pig like grunt call is another interesting facet of these remarkable birds.

The Lake Eyre Island is one of the largest breeding areas in the world of pelicans.

Having crossed Lake Eyre by boat in 1974, I had been toying with the idea of attempting a crossing in 2004 I had flown low across the lake with Malcolm Mitchell from Muloorina, who would have seen more of Lake Eyre from the air over the years than any other man alive. The deep water in the bottom half of the lake would present no problem, but getting to it from the Warburton mouth certainly was. However, as we flew I thought I could see a feasible route in an inflatable boat, eventually running up through the Warburton Groove to the Warburton mouth.

We landed at Mungerannie where I met up with my party. Off down the Warburton, with Bill Oliver on board to take the party back upstream to the vehicles, leaving myself and Nick Brooks to attempt a crossing. Channel nine had agreed to pick us up and lift the outboard and gear across to the shore if we ran out of water. I was very conscious of the fact that it had to be a serious attempt to warrant calling in the chopper.

For the past two days there were fierce nor' westerly winds blowing, and we had a lot of trouble in getting Bill's party off the mouth shore into deep enough water with the two foot waves running. Finally did leaving Nick, Stubbie and I to prepare for our little adventure. We were prepared to push the boat for miles if need be, but I wasn't feeling too confident. We had strapped a blue plastic tarp around the front of the Avon so that it went underneath the boat, across the top, leaving just enough room for the three of us to sit at the back. We had enough hard stores for about five days, and were prepared to live very hard. One would sleep on top of the boat and the other in a blow up "lilo" tied to the side. Stubbie could take his pick, some people might think they should report me to the RSPCA for taking a dog on such an undertaking, but I can tell you this little jack russell would go anywhere, as long as I was there.

We waited impatiently for the wind to drop all morning, but it showed no signs of doing so. Our situation was that if I decided to abort the attempt, I could make it back to the other party before they left in the vehicle at 10a.m. the next day.

So, after lunch at 1p.m., we headed off out along the Warburton Groove into rough water about half a metre deep. We went about two kilometres before running out of navigable water, and mud too deep to push the boat. This didn't really surprise me, and made the decision to turn back at about 2p.m. I would have been surprised however to know that only five kilometres in front of us, there was no water whatsoever, the strong winds had simply blown it out of the so called "groove" across the vast mud flats.

If we put in a lot of travelling time we reckoned we should be able to catch Bill before he left the vehicle camp next morning. I had a satellite phone, but no way could I ring him on that. Also had an UHF radio, but he was out of range.

We headed back through the Warburton, our speed hampered by two foot choppy waves. About dusk we pulled up, having made our way back through the "wetlands". Bill's bamboo sticks with little red flags were still standing where we planted them. This was to help Bill get back through this difficult area. We were almost up to the end of the "top broad water". After a meal and a yarn, we rolled the swags out for an early night, wondering how the camp would have been on the lake if able to continue.

We were up at 4a.m., boiled up the billy and off by 4.30a.m. making good time in the Avon. Every 20 minutes or so we would give Bill a call, but still out of range. The radio in the Oka was switched on.

It was going to be touch and go, but I knew Bill would not leave until exactly 10a.m. even though he wouldn't be expecting us to return. Then, at 9.30a.m. we got an answer which was a relief. We were some two kilometres from the vehicle, and a good sight they were when we rounded the bend.

About 2001 was the last trip, I did down the Warburton, and had an "interesting" trip back to the vehicle, scratching lots of gravel on a rapidly falling river.

In late 2003, the Diamantina ran quite a high flood, but was relatively short lived. In February 2004 I took a party up to do a boat safari. The Cooper was too high at

Innamincka to cross there, so had to drive "around the corner" (Haddon's) to get to our put in spot on Durrie Station.

We had a good trip, once again motoring right into Birdsville; the temperatures were averaging around 47 degrees celsius most days, but being on the river the heat didn't present a problem. We were ahead of the sandflies and only minimal discomfit from flies and mozzies.

We ran into a varied media contingent there and that night Brookie and I (as original secretary and president) were able to organise a rare meeting of the "Green Lizard League". Before I owned the Birdsville Pub, in the summer of 1964, the flooding had caused the pub to run out of beer, but there were stacks of Crème de Menthe and lemonade in the cellar. As a result we had to consistently drink "Green Lizards" – the "Green Lizard League" was a "bullshit" club formed as a result of this (See chapter "Long Hot Summer" in "Mulga Madness", my second book).

Two TV stations sat in on this in the "Green Lizard Bar" at the pub, and we inducted a few more members. They included Joe Fort, one of the present pub owners. The current policeman, the lady flying doctor, TV presenters, our boat crew and a few other locals. Probably enough to keep the club going for another 25 years!

The only other drama I had was an altercation with the local caravan park proprietor, who accused me of landing on caravan park property (for the second time in three years) without official permission! Fair dinkum. Sign of the times. Captain Sturt never had any problems like that – at least not from European Australians.

All this water soon filled Goyders Lagoon Swamp and ran on down the Warburton to Lake Eyre. So, in March and April, I operated three more Warburton trips, making a total of 14 since 1974.

On the first of these, artist Jeff Morgan from Hawker accompanied me. His gallery houses the famous Flinders Ranges Panorama, and his paintings are becoming increasingly well known across the country. Some months later, I was delighted when he presented me with a large painting of my boat rounding a bend with one of the red dramatic Warburton Cliffs in the background.

The ownership of Kalamurina had changed, but I had very good co-operation from Nathan Keogh and his partner, which means a lot when operating in that country.

On both of these trips, the overall bird numbers were dramatically down, probably as a result of the drought. Dingoes, however, were an ever present feature, and on the first trip we counted 43 there. On three different occasions dingoes swam the river in front of the boats, and on one of these, I managed to get a very good series of photographs.

On all trips we were able to camp on "Royal Spoonbill Island" the third one though was memorable for all the wrong reasons.

I had a party comprising an old West Australian station owner mate of ours, Dick Vincent, and his wife, Jan, and a friend of theirs, Tony Proctor. Plus Sue Wood and George Gornagz, who was particularly interested in wildlife. We had a falling river coming down, and I put in a long day in order to make the island taking a gamble on having enough water to make it. We had a number of hold-ups, and consequently it was just after dark when we arrived within 20 metres of the island before running out of water.

Rather than turning around and spending half an hour travelling back to a less interesting "mainland" camp, I elected to camp on the island. This involved a very difficult "slog through the bog", many times to cart our gear in. Not the ideal ending for a long day at the office, but such are the trials and tribulations of Lake Eyre travel. A beautiful setting next morning went a long way toward making up for it. This would have to be one of my more unusual "regular" campsites.

Our second trip down had quite a dramatic island component. Channel Seven TV wanted to meet us there by helicopter and shoot a short documentary. They fixed a rendezvous time on the day that I calculated we would be arriving. It was 4p.m. and we arrived at 4.30p.m. but no chopper. We set up camp expecting an arrival any time, but the sun disappeared into the lake and still no Channel Seven. This was a bit of a concern but nothing we could do about it. Then, right on "last light" a light was spotted to the north. I didn't at first connect this with the helicopter because it was supposed to be coming from Adelaide.

We had a good fire going, and after some time elapsed we heard what was unmistakably a chopper. Next thing it was above, all lights and noise, the down draught blew gear off the table and sand in the tucker, but never mind that. I indicated the only area available to land on our tiny island, the big chopper settled down. A film crew staggered out carrying assorted gear, and introductions were made. Eventually out came the youngest chopper pilot I had ever struck. He looked about 17 in the fire light, but turned out to be 21.

They were all relieved to be "somewhere" having had a long and trying day. They had ended up having to fly by Qantas to Ayers Rock, and hiring a helicopter from there. The young bloke handled it very well, but he was glad to see our fire. Not a lot of street lights around the north end of Lake Eyre.

The crew spent the morning filming finishing off with Martin Tucker and Joseph Bonney getting talked into stripping off and diving out of the boat. This was filmed from the boat and the air, and no doubt gave a few of their more conservative friends and family a rude shock as they viewed their evening TV.

So much for the Warburton for a while. Every Summer I watch rainfall reports in Western Queensland with great interest, hoping once again to knock the cobwebs off my two Stacer punts.

11

The Paroo River

I had my eye on the Paroo River for a number of years waiting for a good flood to run it in the boats. Finally the opportunity presented itself in March 2000.

The Paroo rises in western Queensland, between Quilpie and Charleville, running south through station country (range land or semi desert) to cross the NSW border at Hungerford. It continues in a southerly direction through sheep stations, past the town of Wanaaring, eventually running into a big flood out area. Exceptional floods will sometimes get through to the Darling River.

This looked like being a pretty rough trip, so decided against a "general" type of party. Bill Oliver was coming with me with Tony Bomford (who has no fear of anything) as the only paying member. Another mate, Alby Mangels, was coming to shoot a documentary of the trip. I had Stubbie as usual, and Alby had a large friendly dog of uncertain origins with him. We had my 12 foot Stacer punt with 25 h.p. Johnson outboard, and Alby had a small tinny with a small outboard he was trying out for a sponsor. Tony had his canoe, which I reluctantly gave the okay to bring on the proviso that we may have to abandon it. He is a keen canoeist.

We left in the Oka from my place on the Murray, expecting to be away around eight or nine days. We took a route via Renmark, Wentworth, Menindie, Cobar, Bourke (where we met Tony) and then through to Hungerford. Hungerford is comprised mainly of a gem of a bush pub, well worth the visit. It sits right on the dog fence, which is also the State border. Hungerford is just inside Queensland.

I had arranged to meet a bloke I know from Thargomindah called "Dogger" Dare, and he duly arrived at the pub. The few locals took quite an interest in our intended venture, several making the usual doomsday predictions. I couldn't help thinking they might be right. This river varied somewhat from the true desert rivers. It ran through arid, but higher rainfall country than the Cooper, Diamantina and Georgina Rivers. This meant that there was a lot more thick vegetation in the river, particularly large nepunya gums which had the habit of growing right through the shallower flood out areas.

"Dogger" was a wealth of information concerning the area, being a shearing contractor. He was a big heavily built bloke, with a smiling happy nature and a shock of black curly hair. He was our "back-up" man.

We headed off about mid afternoon and crossed the river through a foot of flowing water over a long causeway. I drove about 10 kilometres up the west side of the river, finally turning into a spot where I intended launching. I walked in, but the timber was so thick, that it was impossible to launch so we reluctantly drove back to the causeway and made camp.

We rolled out the swags and went to bed. About one in the morning I woke up as several vehicles drove into our camp. With much drunken revelry emanating from them. It was a shearing team heading back to their station after a day and night at the Hungerford Pub. Now there is nothing more annoying than being cold sober, half asleep, and being descended on by a mob of drunks. They know no reason, and can be as difficult to get rid of as getting that other stuff off a blanket. Fortunately most of our swags were in the bush a bit away from the vehicle and camp. This was where Dogger performed one of his many good bits of work for us. He jumped out of his swag and "engaged" the drunks. They all knew him, and most had worked for him as well.

Dogger skilfully handled their "bullshit", and within half an hour they were back in their vehicles and off on their way to a day of bleary eyes and hangovers. We all subsided back into peaceful slumber, with only the regular call of the boobook owl to disturb us.

Next morning we drove to the edge of the causeway, and began unloading my punt, Alby's boat and Tony's canoe off the top of the Oka. Stores, outboard and camp gear from out of the back. We tied the boats to the truck while we packed them, and were all set to go. When I looked for my hat it was no where to be found, and I could only surmise that it must have been knocked off the tailgate and headed off down the swiftly flowing river. I was not very happy, your hat is part of you, particularly when it is "worn in", and to be parted from it is to feel half-naked. I was very unhappy. I had to make do with an evil orange towelling arrangement until a few days later Dogger bought me in an old bush hat belonging to the publican. This did improve my demeanour a fair bit.

The three craft headed off in the fast flowing water through lignum and timber, finding enough room to manoeuvre. In less than an hour we came to the dog fence and State border, and here we were held up. The fence showed about two foot above the water forming a very effective barrier. It is illegal to interfere in any way with the dingo proof fence with large fines applying, however we had to get through. After travelling up and down it, I could see there was no easy way through it, so we pulled up and I cut a section out of it, just big enough to get the boat through it. When we were in NSW I wired it back up to be as good as new.

I should say it's a very rare occurrence for boat traffic to have had to resort to such measures.

After negotiating some heavy timber, we pulled up on an island about a quarter acre in size to boil the billy for lunch. The mood was good; we were well on our way with high hopes of a successful trip.

In the afternoon though we had the first of our many dramas. The river varied from very shallow water with wide flood outs, to fast flowing stretches where we were completely blocked by nepunya gums (this species supports a localised honey industry, as its nectar is very sought after by apiarists). Sometimes we would need to find a way around them, often running into shallow water before we did. We were lucky with this particular flood, if it had been much higher, we would have had to travel through the branches and foliage of the Nepunyas, a task that I think would have made travel impossible. If the flood was much lower we would have been stranded in many sections by shallow water. As it was we spent a lot of time dragging the boats through lignum swamps with only a foot or so of water.

By contrast we had some excellent sections through the waterholes. Birdlife was good and we had many sightings of the large red winged parrots, always a pleasure to see.

We were now in sheep country, which brought its own hazard of fences. In many cases the flood washes them out. But not always by a long shot. We would normally get no warning before we were into one, sometimes the boat hitting with its keel, and sometimes the outboard motor. We had to cut a number of wires with the pliers. One cyclone fence held us up for an hour, having to cut it off the propeller under water.

We were very glad to actually find some dry land to camp on that first night, emerging from a waterhole on to a wide flood out with very shallow water. Ended up dragging the boats nearly a kilometre to a nice sandy little flat on the eastern shore. It was an excellent camp.

The next three days were full of varied experiences. Tony was tipped out of his canoe twice, all of which didn't upset him, one iota. But after he shot over a barb wire fence, which nearly bought him undone, he decided to come on board "the mother ship". We left his canoe on shore at a lunch camp. There were a couple of water board blokes taking river measurements, and we had lunch with them.

This was one of the spots that Dogger was able to get in to meet us, so we had a long lunch hour. We were soon off again, the pattern was that Alby would follow close behind Bill, Tony and I in the Stacer punt filming us. This he did with great professionalism, even when we could have used his assistance in trouble spots. But, he is the true professional cameraman. At times Bill and I would curse him, badly needing help, but to no avail. And just as well, because he recorded some very good action footage. I had never been down a river like this before; being more used to the generally open desert country. Our roof tarp was in tatters, and the very solid framework had a bend in it where we had collided with a big nepunya gum. The boat was constantly being filled with debris from vegetation, necessitating a constant chucking out of twigs, branches and leaves. Even a bird's nest on occasion.

This was a 25h.p. motor, a bit bigger than my usual Yamaha 15h.p., and I was very grateful for that extra power. We would be swept down fast flowing narrow channels through the lignum, eventually encountering a log across it, or a dead end. On these occasions I would simply give the motor full revs and spear through and sometimes across the top of lignum into another channel, making even Stubbie hang on.

On occasions we were literally airborne. Some of the lignum had sand humps up through them, and these would spear us up into the air before landing with a great splash into another channel. Very exciting I have to say on one such "launch" we landed on top of a large lignum bush with no water under us, which meant 10 minutes hard labour man handling the boat back to water. This was the only way I could make headway in a lot of this swamp country. It is only a pity that most of this really dramatic stuff took place on the couple of days that Alby was absent.

Dogger had picked him up to go and organise a pastoralist's plane, so that he could get some aerial shots of the boats and river. However it was just as well because his little light boat and small outboard couldn't have followed over all that lignum. As it was Alby's big dog came a gutser quite often as he couldn't seem to find his "sea legs". Would often look back and see him swimming down the channel behind Alby's boat. Once he tried to board Tony's canoe, a day or two earlier, only to receive one hell of a tongue lashing in Tony's precise English. Tony was having enough trouble staying upright without being boarded by an eight stone dog!

In between there were periods of very peaceful travel, down long channels, through beautiful long wide waterholes and some flood plain with some quite deep water. There were wild pigs and numerous red kangaroos.

Once we came across a small sand spit with 12 sheep on it. They had been there a while, and had eaten it bare, even the bark off the small trees. I sent Stubbie overboard, and he chased them off the sand spit through a hundred metres of shallow water to the far bank. He came back very pleased with himself It was the first time he was legitimately allowed to chase sheep and in this case it saved their lives. I think he might have some kelpie genes, because I can actually work him sheep dog fashion behind a mob of camels, they take no notice, but the little bloke reckons he does a good job.

I was looking for and recognised an old 4WD camp of mine, where I had camped a couple of years previously on one of my 30 day "transcontinental" safaris. We had spent a good day there catching a feed of fish.

There was one camp where we had to pick-up Alby and meet Dogger. He told us to look out for a red 12 gallon drum in a tree. Well we never saw the drum, and I switched the motor off drifting and giving some cooees. There was a sort of water logged cooee, and we spied Dogger's head of curly black hair coming towards us out of a channel.

Realising we would probably miss the drum; he started swimming out toward the sound of our outboards, ripping bits of his shirt and tying them onto lignum. These were his markers to get him back out again if he missed us. That's what I called dedication.

On the fifth day we came to Wonaaring, and parking the boats we walked a kilometre or so into the pub and had a counter lunch. When we told the barman we had come down the river, he just gave us a funny look and said nothing. I guess some people try and avoid a cluttered mind. After lunch we negotiated one of the thickest areas of timber. It covered a maze of channels and I thought we would never get through it. Often had to back track, but finally one channel led us out into better travelling. Couple of hours later, we came on to a beautiful waterhole and spied Dogger's "holiday camp" where our trip was to end. He rented this little station, using it as a fishing camp. From here the Paroo becomes a maze of channels, finally running out on to a big flood out. Dogger and Alby were there to meet us and Dogger had a fridge full of yellow belly and beer. We pulled the boats out of the water, and hosed the debris out and loaded them on to the Oka.

We had a very funny evening of fish, beer and yarning. Dogger cooked a magnificent meal; we had travelled over 100 kilometres down this interesting river. There is talk of damming it for cotton growing, but let's hope common sense prevails and it is left as a wild river. Next morning Bill, Alby and I headed off in the Oka for Broken Hill, and Dogger and Tony went back to Hungerford.

The boat trip had taken five days.

12

Down a Desert River – Kallakoopah Creek to Lake Eyre

I have been operating desert boat safaris since 1966, which is all about waiting for above normal rains in the catchment of these rivers, and then striking while the iron is hot. There is very often only a short window of opportunity to get a party together, drive to the location, do the trip and get out before your river runs out of water. Such is the nature of desert rivers.

The operating risk, both physical and financial are considerable, but I would rate my desert boat safaris over the years, above anything else I have done in commercial safaris, including 4WD vehicles and camels. Floating through a pristine desert environment with wall to wall birdlife, sometimes good fishing, the world's best campsites and total isolation from other people.

Probably, our most significant desert voyages have been down the Warburton and Cooper Rivers to Lake Eyre in 1974, when Lake Eyre filled for the first and only time in white man's memory.

For a number of years I had contemplated doing a boat trip down the full length of the Kallakoopah Creek from where it leaves the Warburton to where it rejoins it 10kms from Lake Eyre. This true desert watercourse only runs a full channel on rare occasions, depending on high flood conditions in the Warburton to overflow across a large sand bar area at the beginning of the Kallakoopah. This is a huge Anabranch of the Warburton. It heads out a long way north into the southern part of the Simpson Desert before turning west then south to rejoin the Warburton.

In April of 2000 we flew the length of the Kallakoopah which was "educational". At first glance, flying over some of these flooded rivers is pretty daunting. They are often miles wide, a maze of channels, swamps and flood outs, and certainly makes the undertaking even more of a challenge. You sometimes get a few valuable clues, but mostly have little value when you are down there amidst it in the boats.

I had a tentative party standing by and I made the decision to go about three weeks before the departure date.

The river was holding its own and provided I could get underway before it began dropping at its source, where it left the Warburton we would hopefully have enough water.

A couple of major preoccupations were the large shallow lakes about half way along its course.

Either of these could bring us undone, and if this happened I would have to get a helicopter in to lift people out, a very expensive undertaking. The boats, motors, and much of the gear would have to be left until I could get in there with 4WD vehicles – another expensive proposition.

On May 26, eight of us and my jack russell terrier (Stubbie) arrived on the Warburton at a point 15kms from Cowarie Station homestead. Cowarie and Kalamurina are the two big desert cattle stations whose country most of the Warburton/Kallakoopah complex flows through. The owners and managers of these runs have been very helpful to me over the years. In this case the Cowarie manager, John Germain would drive my Oka 4WD to another location on Kalamurina, the point that I planned on returning to in the boats, but first we had to negotiate the unknown channels and lakes of the Kallakoopah.

We spent the usual couple of hours sorting out the boats, packing away drums of outboard fuel, stores (and grog) to sustain eight people for a fortnight, if need be. Swags, bags and much miscellaneous gear from satellite phone to long handle shovel.

The boats were the extra heavy duty Stacer flat-bottomed, aluminium punts with flared bow, one 12 feet and one 14 feet. Also an Avon inflatable. Both punts had their usual canvas canopies.

Our party was a diverse one, all but one of them having travelled with me before. My mate, Bill Oliver was the other punt boatman. He is a McLaren Vale farmer and flyer. Matt Riley, another mate from Burra, an ex station man and bush contractor. Daryl Wallace, a horticulturist from Melbourne. Our only female member, Fran Bush from Budgewoi in NSW. Stavros Pippos, a well known landscape photographer. Tony Bomford, a retired English Army surveyor, in his 70's, our oldest member and probably one of the fittest. Finally David Suckling, a sculptor from NSW, and the youngest in the party.

After an early lunch we pushed off the sand hill and headed upstream in the Warburton against a current of around five kilometres an hour. Our speed was six to seven kilometres per hour against it. Always a very exciting moment when the boats actually head off, very much into an unknown situation on this occasion. There was a very real possibility that if we couldn't get our boats over the sandbar at the start of the Kallokoopah, we would have to abort the whole expedition after a couple of days.

This particular part of the Warburton is probably the most un-interesting part of the Warburton in my opinion. Quite a wide river (approx. 120m) with a shoreline of stunted timber and undergrowth, unlike further downstream.

The birds were active however, and one highlight was coming across a black breasted buzzard on the nest.

We reached what I thought was the smaller channel (20m wide) that should have been our entry into the waters of the Kallakoopah late in the afternoon, making camp among some river coobah. Soon after Darren and I took off in the Avon to see if we could get through, and only made about 200m through shallow water, before it was impossible to travel further. We returned to camp with the unwelcome news, and then headed back out to the Warburton and travelled slowly up the heavily timbered (coolibah and coobah) northern bank, looking for an opening in the fast fading light. We were just about to give it away when we spied a very small opening some 300m from our camp. It was only metres wide as we idled our way in. It led out on to a large body of water with dead coolibah and scattered lignum, we continued on through water only 18 inches to two foot deep, before the light made it impossible to go further. We turned around and not without some difficulty found our way back to the Warburton. It was completely dark by the time we spied the large fire and smelt the steak cooking. We had a good camp with plenty of speculating about tomorrow, as there was no guarantee we would be able to "get into our river".

We were up before 7a.m. next morning and soon began picking our way across the open water toward a line of timber that I hoped was the channel leading into the Kallakoopah. After about three kilometres we ran out of water for the punts. Darren and I headed off in the Avon and soon found a boggy looking shallow channel that headed about 300m to a line of heavy timber. We managed to get through with some difficulty, snags a bit of pushing here and there, before coming to a very narrow channel of fast flowing deep water. I was very happy with this as it could be the conduit we needed to get us to the main river.

We returned to the party, on foot, and began the laborious job of pushing and pulling the heavily loaded punts through shallow water and mud half a metre deep. It took us a good two hours of heavy work to get to the Avon on the edge of the channel. The mature coolibahs signified it was a major channel and everyone's morale lifted considerably. But it was very narrow, averaging around three to four metres, and I was concerned about large trees blocking it. This problem had prevented passage in the past.

We put the boats in, and there began a couple of very exciting hours where we could have easily come unstuck. The current propelled us at a fast rate down the winding channel, and Bill had to take a lot of care he didn't crash into me when I was often pulled up around a corner. There was dense lignum, with a big white sand dune on the west side of the channel. There was one log right across we cut with the axe. Sometimes the channel split, and Darren would take great delight in jumping into the river and swimming or wading to check it out. Then we came up against a massive coolibah log right across the channel that had probably been there since Charles Sturt poked across these flats. Everyone stretched their legs, and Stubbie and I did a recce along the top of a sand hill, disturbing a wedgetailed eagle off his nest in a high dead coolibah. It was all sand hills to the west, which was s good sign. I could see by the timberline that our channel continued on to the north, and to the east there was water as far as the eye could see. Small as this channel was, it must be the one, and it just seemed too little an amount of water to constitute the Kallakoopah. On the way back from a high vantage point I could see at least one yellow eaglet in the "wedgies" nest, and soon after the eagle soared low above Stubbie having a good look at him. Bit of a worry those wedgetails – I've seen them contemplate jack russell's on a few occasions, but they have always given them a miss. Little silky terriers have been taken to my knowledge. I must say Stubbie didn't seem to share my concern.

Back to the boats and 10 minutes pushing and pulling had us through the lignum and around the log and back into deep water. Bit lucky there. After a bit more scrub bashing with people often having to lay low, the channel suddenly ran out into a big flood out, and using the GPS we were able to keep our general direction. All flow had ceased and we had between two and three feet of water under us. Still a bit of a worry, and the thought of having to return over our route, didn't have a lot of appeal.

After half an hour I noticed a gap in some timber and this turned out to be another channel. This one was wider and we felt more comfortable with it. The last half hour across the flat and in the new channel was an absolute feast of bird life. We identified seven duck species including mountain ducks, raptors including goshawk, little falcons and black breasted buzzard, black winged stilts, red necked avocets, a pair of tawny frogmouths and many more.

About midday we pulled up to an acre of mud that we called an island. It had two dead coolibahs on it, and would serve nicely for lunch. Stubbie immediately ran over and ran up a diagonal branch (he's a tree climbing dog) and a pair of boobook owls flew out to complete our bird bonanza.

It was a jovial lunch. We felt that we were past the point of no return.

We continued on down a good fast flowing channel about 20m wide and after an hour came to the abandoned Mona Downs Outstation. This was an outpost of Cowarie out in the Simpson Desert, and surely one of the most isolated homesteads in the country. We pulled in for half an hour and there was plenty of interest. The inevitable clump of Athol pines, a sure sign of European settlement in this part of the world. It was earlier supposed that this was the only tree that would grow with Artesian bore water, but Brian Powell among others disproved this theory. The old homestead foundations were still evident; a couple of old fowl sheds and the remains of pig pens built from heavy coolibah. Some old farm machinery including a harrow and seed drill. They often used to grow lucerne for the horses. Apparently this was as far as the river reached during some floods, rarely running on down to the lake. Leaving there, we very definitely put behind us the last remnants of European civilisation. The channel became fast flowing again with lots of big snags, and it was pretty exciting travel, with Bill again having to exercise a lot of care around some sharp bends in case I was pulled up. Matt, Darren and David took it in turns to operate the Avon inflatable bringing up the rear. Once more out onto a huge flat with scattered lignum and coolibah, Tony (the ex-army surveyor) had taken on the role of official navigator and was meticulous in his use of the map and GPS. I always rely on water flow and general direction, but GPS's have certainly made my life easier.

I was very aware that we had to avoid a large channel that would take us some 40 or so kilometres back to the Warburton. It was very difficult to pick this in the flood conditions and the GPS was invaluable here. We actually had to back track a couple of kilometres because we had unknowingly entered it without realising it.

That night camp was on a fast flowing channel with the water only six inches below the top of the bank. It wasn't a "bad day at the office" you might say, and that night I rang John Germain at Cowarie to tell him it was okay to move the Oka – we weren't coming back!

Next day was one of good travelling, mostly in a defined channel, and averaging 10-12kms an hour. We saw a grey falcon mid morning, one of our rarer raptors, and other birdlife was of constant interest.

I noticed at the camp the previous night that Stubbie had lost his colourful woollen coat that Matt had bought with him, and someone said they saw it on him when he ran down a rabbit warren at the old outstation. When he re-appeared it was no longer on him – so much for Riley's present! The mornings were particularly cold this trip, travelling in the boat, with the sun quite often appearing around mid morning.

While we were having lunch, Darren gave a yell from 100m up river. We went up to him, and sticking out of the riverbank half a metre was a huge bone. Several others could be seen partly covered. Far too big for cattle or camels, so had to be in prehistoric league, we took a number of photographs and a later report from the South Australian Museum confirmed the bones as belonging to a Diprotoden. They thought that it was part of an intact skeleton which made the find even more interesting. We gave them the co-ordinates and hopefully one day they will go out and have a look.

Stubbie meanwhile had disappeared down some rabbit warrens, and sitting down drinking our tea, we saw him making his way down from some high ground carrying something in his mouth. Several times he disappeared from sight, reappearing out of deep gutters, and obviously in "low range four legged drive", scratching his way up the steep sides of the cutters. Finally he trotted down through the lunch camp and leapt onto the front of my boat. He had a half-grown dead sandy rabbit in his jaws, which he must have killed down the burrow and for a change bought it up. Probably didn't know where his next feed was coming from.

Much of this country was now totally devoid of coolibahs and we felt like we were very definitely in a desert river. Late that afternoon we came to a large un-named lake, our next potential hazard. We camped on a large flat covered in mitre bush, a low spreading plant that has a small blackish fruit much sought after by major mitchell cockatoos in particular, although they didn't occur here. That day we travelled a distance of 80kms, our best to date. We were carrying some firewood and managed to get some more here as there were a few dead coolibahs. The nights were cold enough but up until about 9.30a.m. most people were still wearing gloves. If this trip had a downside it was the overcast cold mornings, particularly in the boats.

Such was the case next morning as we motored through an opening out of the channel on to the lake. There was a nice breeze from the south west, throwing up a few waves that didn't add to our comfort. Earlier on we had about a metre of water and judging by the map we had to get around the back of several small mud islands in the middle. They were visible, having a bit of low mitre bush on them. The lake was probably around 5,000 acres in area. Very soon we ran out of water, and most of us were over the side pushing and suffering from the freezing water. Fran always offered, but not being what you call a "physical" person, she was always allowed to stay in the boat. She made up for her physical contributions by her very considerable efforts in the food area. She was a lady you could take anywhere.

We scouted around a bit in the Avon looking for a bit of depth, mostly these lakes have channels of some kind through them, but they were very elusive in this one. Dragging and pushing the boats through six inches of water and a foot of mud between the islands was hard going, but apart from our frozen feet the manual labour got the rest of us warmed up. After awhile we struck deeper water, just enough to travel in with our outboard's right up. A long brown muddy lake marked our passage. All of a sudden Bill, who was walking behind his boat, went down to his waist, giving a few interesting exclamations. We were in water that we couldn't depth with a long handled shovel, in the middle of the lake, pulled up and recorded a pre-arranged interview with the ABC on my satellite phone. We called this Lake Delusion.

About mid afternoon we reached the most northerly part of the Kallakoopah, so it was south and all "downhill" from here.

We collected some wood from a stand of dead coolibah over half a kilometre from the river, and made floating "eagle nests" of the boats. Soon after we pulled into a lovely little inlet and a perfect camp at the base of a big white sand dune. Stavros headed off along the short setting up his camera for the special landscape photographs he specialises in. On many occasions he comes back without having tripped his shutter release, but such is the nature of his craft. He was currently working on a book called "The shades of Ochre" which turned out to be a great success.

Away by 6.25a.m. next morning a day of exquisite riverine scenery. Extremely arid, very few trees with the occasional spectacular sand and gypsum cliffs up to around 70 feet high. In one of these we observed a barn owl standing at the entrance to a hole in the cliffs, six metres above water level. It allowed us to drift in below the hole and some good photography was had. My Nikon 400mm anti-vibration lens did justice to the situation, and Stavros used one of his photographs on the back cover of "The Shades of Ochre". We videoed this event as we had been during the entire expedition, little realising that the borrowed camera was faulty, meaning we ended up without a video record of this trip. A big disappointment.

Quite often you see galahs, little corellas and kestrels nesting in the numerous holes in the cliffs, and I have seen barn owls before on the Warburton and Cooper.

This river really now was taking on the aspect of a "live artery in a dead heart" for about 10kms we had a series of white dunes free of vegetation running into the river. The initial flood had cut them off like a knife through hot butter, and left them as very dominant features on the landscape.

Dingoes were conspicuous by their absence, which was surprising as you would normally see and hear plenty of them. I put it down to the fact that there was so much country enjoying good seasons throughout the inland that they were getting plenty to eat away from water.

That night we had what we reckoned was our most desolate camp, but that was no problem.

Next morning we came to a place that concerned me most of all. A large area indicated as swamp on the map and about 12kms across. We took a line across the middle and very soon encountered water a foot deep. It was impossible to walk in it without sinking another foot in soft mud. We ploughed around in the Avon looking for depth, but it was touch and go. If we did have to abandon the expedition here, it would mean having to cart all the gear over half a kilometre to the nearest shore. Just walking through the mud was quite a feat leave alone lugging gear. Eventually though we managed better progress with people pushing.

After floundering along for a good one and a half hours, we suddenly struck deep water and motored for the last four kilometres to the other side of the lake where we enjoyed lunch on top of a big white dune with a good view over the lake.

Even though we would sometimes spend the whole morning in the boats without landing, it didn't present a problem. These Stacer punts are very stable and people can stand up anytime they feel like it leaning on the steel framework, both front and the bow are covered in for a metre, then the front seat has a padded foam cover taking two people. Next is the cargo area, drums of fuel on the bottom, with swags on top of them, then people's personal bags. On the floor at the rear of the fuel are large polythene tubs containing our stores, also the lunch box, two blue waterproof "barrels" for valuable gear, with the post hole shovel lying down one side. Camp stools and table on the opposite side. Under the front is a miscellaneous cargo of two-stroke oil, axe, bow saw, rope, cask wine etc. The rear thwart has two boat seats mounted on it. The framework of steel tube has a canvas canopy which can be folded back front and back if required, we sometimes put our afternoon load of firewood up there when required and Stubbie quite often uses it as a hammock. Our load per boat at the beginning of these trips is around the tonne, but this still gives us a good nine inches of freeboard.

Not long after lunch we came to the mouth of the Macumba River, which was only about 25m wide, and immediately grounded in a great mass of silt, all hands out pushing and luckily we cleared it in a short distance. Our channel was now only about 15m across and very meandering, and we knew that we had almost made it. We had constant groundings on big gobs of silt, but the fast flowing water helped us get free. I recognised very familiar landmarks (dunes) on the Warburton across the other side of the big floodout. The pelican population increased dramatically since the mouth of the Macumba, squadrons of them were on every sand spit, with many hundreds soaring above. No matter how many pelicans you see, enough is never enough. We would often pass within metres of them with many not taking to the wing.

Finally motored out of the Kallakoopah into the Warburton around 4p.m. and a good moment for us all. There are two entrances into the Warburton; one being a narrow channel of about a kilometre, this heads off to the left and a broader reach to the right that we took. This merges with the Warburton in a broad body of water about half a kilometre wide.

I then took off with Stavros in the Avon to try and reach the mouth of the Warburton with enough light for photography. It was a distance of 10kms over a stretch of water I know very well. Planing along at about 30km/h it didn't take too long. As we approached the mouth a helicopter approached from the direction of the lake with a camera man sitting in the open doorway hanging his legs out. We heard later that it was an ABC film crew, and we were apparently included when it came out. I often wondered if they realised where we had come from. We landed a kilometre from the mouth and I accompanied Stavros up to a high point overlooking the lake. A fast walk of about 20 minutes and although I have looked at this sight about a dozen times, it never loses its magic. Different every time, a dramatic sunset always a bonus. A great body of water flowed out on to the lake with big areas of mud and salt either side of it. The water was essentially in the "Warburton groove" and it's only when the lake was completely full (as in 1974) would all the lake be covered with water.

This was Stavros' second visit here having been with me on a Warburton boat safari the year before, and this time he was successful in getting the shot he was after (the one depicted in "The Shades of Ochre").

By the time we had walked back down to the camp, Bill and Matt had a fire going and dinner on, and an excellent camp it was, with a bit to celebrating going on. As he had done on other occasions, Darren produced a bottle of vintage port from his gear.

There's something about drinking quality wine in arid locations. We had four days to travel back up the Warburton to the Oka.

First thing next morning I took most of the party out to what I call "Royal Spoonbill Island", spent an hour or so on it and the lake and back to my "Lake Eyre" camp. Loading up, we headed off around 10a.m. on our long haul back up the Warburton, a distance of 140 kilometres. It is obviously slower against he current and you really have to put the hours in. Back up through the choppy "broad water" to the channels, and the trickiest part of the Warburton changing as it does all the time.

We didn't have too much trouble on this occasion, and I experienced the usual relief when we emerged out on to the top "broad water" which runs for some 12kms.

The timber was much appreciated as usual when it reappeared, and after a good day's travel we camped on the Simpson Desert bank.

That night I cooked my special cabbage dish, and we made a great effort to almost force feed Matt, as he hates cabbage. Let it be noted that protesting loudly, he took a lot of cabbage on board.

In the morning we were up at 4.30a.m. and away in the boats by 6a.m. completely enveloped in a dense fog. It was Matt's turn in the Avon and I told him to, make sure he kept up, otherwise could get lost in the fog. Bill in the second boat would keep an eye on him (we used rear vision mirrors), but Matt would only have been a smudge in the distance. We travelled for two and half hours before going ashore to warm up and attend to our toilets – all except Matty. When he pulled up his face was quite pale and did he have a tale (tail) to tell! It was to do with cabbage and sensitive squeamish readers may choose to skip this bit. Soon after we headed off into the fog, Matty felt a few rumbles down below. He tried to put it out of his mind and concentrate on keeping Bill's boat in sight in the fog. Then to his horror, he realised that would have to . . . "go". What a dilemma. He wasn't game to go ashore in case Bill hadn't realised that he had stopped in the fog. Now, Riley is a bushman of great resourcefulness. He had been in worse predicaments, so decided to "go" while he was at full throttle in the Avon. With one hand he managed to lower his daks and long johns, then he hang his derriere over the back (a shocking sight for any Warburton marine life) and "went" in a big way. He even raised the prop to create some turbulence eliminating the need for toilet paper, but almost eliminating something else in the process. A very tricky manoeuvre for the most athletic amongst us, bearing in mind he had the boat at full throttle, not daring to take his eyes off Bill's boat.

Thinking that was the end of it and feeling pretty pleased with himself, he got himself together again. However one should never underestimate the fearful repercussions of a night out on the cabbage. Half and hour later, the terrible truth dawned on him that he was going to have to repeat the process again! This time, however, it wasn't what you would call a clean-cut operation. I don't intend to go into details here, but things didn't go quite to plan, and there was a "clean up" required. Suffice to say that a combination of mobility (travelling fast through the water) and turbulence caused by the outboard had a lot to do with his seemingly successful laundry operation, and by the look of his white face, that must have been through the process as well. He had certainly "done a day's work" by the time he pulled up. So had we by the time the mirth subsided.

Several more days of typical Warburton River with spectacular cliffs and riverine scenery.

On the last camp, Matt did have a bit of a win. We built the fire at the base of a Coolibah stump about five metres high and took bets as to when it would fall over. It finally did at 2a.m. and Matt's guess was the closest, so he won some little treasure. I think it was half a packet of peanuts, which after 11 days in boats is of quite high value.

Next day we reached the welcome sight of the Oka, good to see anytime, but especially so this time. It was a trip of a lifetime and everyone experienced a great sense of achievement. Where else in the world can you do 600kms by boat through two deserts?

13

The Coorong

South Australia's Coorong, on the end of the Murray River system is a unique waterway – in the true sense of the word.

It runs for about 120 kilometres south east from the Murray Mouth, with the wilderness sand dune region of the Younghusband Peninsula dividing it from the magnificent 90 Miles Beach and the Southern Ocean.

A dying waterway, in the geological sense, it is of enormous value to Australia as a Ramsar site, giving it international recognition as a wetland region of major importance. It's one of Australia's major wader feeding areas, and the State's largest permanent pelican breeding site.

For thousands of years the local Ngarrindgeri Aborigines lived in the area with an abundance of food, and their descendants are still there. European agriculture has put added pressures on the Coorong. Particularly with the draining of the south east swamps out to sea, a disgraceful waste of valuable freshwater. This once ran into the Coorong providing that unique mix of salt and freshwater that is vital for the health of this waterway. Decreased flooding of the Murray is a very real and ongoing problem.

Despite these factors, the Coorong is still a fascinating and delightful region with a wealth of flora and fauna. Since the late 1970's I have operated a number of Coorong boat safaris, usually around six days duration, using Avon and Zodiak inflatables, and also various "tinnies". Like our desert boat trips, canopies are used as the summer temperatures can sometimes exceed 40 degrees celsius on the Coorong.

Our aim on each trip is to get as far down the Coorong as possible, giving people the most comprehensive experience available. Depth of water will determine how far we go, and every trip had been different. In the 1980's we did a family trip, using the Zodiak and had no trouble getting down to Salt Creek, these boats are ideal, drafting practically no water. Their main drawback though is the possibility of puncturing them on the sharp coral like outcrops that abound.

In early 2002, I operated what was my "shortest" Coorong trip and it happened this way.

It was a seven day itinerary and incorporating the lakes as well. A couple of Melbourne ladies (who I can take anywhere!) arrived at the camel farm on the Murray, staying overnight in the "swaghouse" in the Mallee on top of the cliffs. A mate, Darren Wallace also arrived and next morning we headed south in the Oka with an Avon inflatable and a 12 foot flat bottomed punt on a trailer.

I drove down to Jockwar Station on Lake Alexandrina, owned by another friend (Brenton Hicks and made camp among willows on the lakeshore.

Lake Alexandrina is the largest freshwater lake in the southern hemisphere, and notorious for its "erratic behaviour". With this in mind, I organised the loading so that if the punt was swamped, our "bridges wouldn't be burnt" and it is just as well I did.

The first day, we left the camp intact, and headed off in the Avon around the lake to where the Murray runs in by Brinkley Station Homestead. After lunch, we headed on up river to Wellington and spent some time in the small museum before returning to our camp. Nearby is Wellington Lodge Station, another of the historic lakes sheep stations. On the lakeshore is one of the most remarkable structures in South Australia. Standing around 50 feet in height is an old wooden water tower, and I think of it as South Australia's "Leaning Tower of Pisa", as it has a very definite "lean". Holding around 30,000 gallons (135,000 litres) pumped from the lake; the water was piped inland for irrigated pastures. It is said that the original owner would sit up the top observing his workers. One modern day use is as a nocturnal navigation beacon. A very interesting landmark.

Next day after lunch we motored out past the wooden tower, before changing course for Pomanda Island, another important lake landmark, and haven from high winds. This "island" sits at the southern end of a narrow reed bed stretching about four kilometres from the western shore. When the lake waters are not too high, cattle can walk out to the island which is approximately two hundred acres in area. On the island is an abandoned homestead and when we arrived there were half a dozen cattle occupying the front verandah. For a number of years a Mrs. Agnes Woodrow lived here, surely one of the most isolated homesteads in the "inside country" of South Australia.

Around the north eastern side of the island is "Port Agnes", a haven from bad weather and used by paddle steamers before they crossed the lake. We made a camp at Sandy Beach on the southern side of the island and had a walk around it. The cliffs on the west side provided a good opportunity to chuck large rocks at the huge European carp, but without much success. The noxious boxthorn had recently been bulldozed and burnt, a plant very difficult to eradicate.

While there I saw a very large grey kangaroos that hopped off towards the reed beds. The bird watching was quite good near the reeds with black winged stilts and crested grebes being of interest. Soon after returning to camp, Brenton Hicks and son Tom from Jockwar arrived with a few beers on his jet ski. I am no lover of jet skis but the beers were very welcome.

Next morning we headed off early for a point on the east side of the lake. Although wind can arrive at any time it is usually calm in the mornings, and I was taking advantage of this. I had the two ladies with me in the Avon, which was virtually unsinkable and Darren followed in the punt with cargo that wouldn't "ruin" with a ducking. I knew Darren didn't mind the challenge.

We did about 12 kilometres across open water. During the last 20 minutes a light wind got up but was no problem for us. We ran along the coast about a hundred metres off shore, passing the large homestead complex of Poltalloch, another famous lakes station. A magnificent double storey homestead surrounded by numerous other homesteads and outbuildings. Pulled in for a walk soon after, and had to face the bows of the boats seaward to avoid water over the backs, as the wind had increased.

Continued on to Point Malcolm and its interesting lighthouse. This leads into the narrows and Lake Albert with the little town of Narrung a couple of kilometres distance on the other side.

We pulled in and had lunch near the lighthouse, with a very picturesque outlook. It also happened to be my 60th birthday and Darren produced a small birthday cake and an earthenware container of Rutherglen Tawny Port with a turquoise parrot decorating its outside. A very nice gesture and a memorable lunch.

After lunch we continued on past the ferry and into the narrows. There are huge reed beds there and we had an enjoyable cruise with numerous mountain duck and cape barron geese in evidence.

It was quite hot and we pulled into a small beach on the north side on the channel erecting a tarp, as there was no other shade. Camped for a couple of hours and enjoyed a swim before pushing on down the channel to make camp on the north side near the opening into Lake Albert. Although only about a third of the size of Lake Alexandrina it is still a large lake. The town of Meningie was approximately 16 kilometres distance.

There was a very strong wind blowing and we were grateful for several stunted boxthorns and set up camp behind one of these. This country was once covered in sheoaks (casuarina allocasuaarina) but these proved easy to clear in the early days and very few survived. Consequently the shores of these lakes are practically devoid of trees, with the exception of the dreaded boxthorn.

Our campfire comprised dead boxthorn that burns with a fair amount of heat. It blew a gale through the night. I checked the boats once and they were okay, but in the morning the punt had a lot of water in it.

The wind didn't let up all day, so we didn't' move. Did a bit of walking and read books.

Next day the wind had dropped, so we loaded up and headed back up the narrows to the Narrung Pier. Tying up there we walked into the township and bought some fuel and other items. A local bloke ran us back to the boats and we headed off.

Around past the old Pt. McLeay Aboriginal settlement, along cliffs for the first time, and had lunch on a nice sandy beach, the wind got up again in the afternoon and about 3p.m. we pulled behind a rocky point where there was a bit of protection. There was a long reedy island between us and the self-operating lock on Tauwitcherie Barrage where we would enter the Coorong.

The billy was boiled while we waited for the wind to drop which it did about 4p.m. It looked good so we headed off to the island, about four kilometres distance. After about 10 minutes a stiff wind got up creating two foot waves. Darren's boat (the punt) was taking in water over the front, so I yelled out to head back to shore. I could see Darren was having trouble. His boat was now sitting lower in the water, and with a following sea he was taking in water over the back. Then the punt suddenly foundered and Darren stood up on the swags with no where to go. We were only about half a kilometre off the shore; I shot back there in the inflatable and unloaded the girls and a bit of gear. Then, back out to Darren who was sitting on the half submerged punt.

We loaded the wet swags into my boat. There was a bit of gear floating off, so I loaded Darren and we managed to pick up most of the gear, and took it back to shore. From the shore, I could see that the punt had turned over and was drifting in the wind with the canopy frame slowing it down. There was about four feet of water there. Darren and I went out again and took the punt in tow, but found that the frame and the 9h.p. Yamaha outboard had come off. The outboard had a tie rope on it, but it must have broken, which surprised me.

We pulled the swags apart and spread all the bedding over bushes. It was very good drying weather, which was one thing in our favour.

Early next morning Darren and I spent an hour dragging the lake bottom but were unable to locate either the frame or the outboard.

Then we loaded up and taking the punt in tow headed off for the island once more, on calm water. Reaching that, we rounded the northern end, and motored down to Tauwitcherie Barrage. I didn't go through the self-operating lock as we only had another day here. Instead I camped at the southern end of the long barrage. We manhandled the Avon over into the Coorong, spending the afternoon on the Coorong and across on Younghusband Peninsula. The bird watching from our camp was very good, with a dozen species of waders being present, some in big numbers. Next morning, Brenton arrived in my Oka; we loaded up and returned to Jockwar.

Previous trips have followed a pattern of travelling, idyllic camps on the narrow beaches of Younghusband Peninsula, walks through to the ocean gathering cockles – both to eat and for bait. Fishing for the delicious Coorong mullet, and of course, bird watching. Mirages are a real feature of the Coorong, and a never-ending source of interest.

In January 2003, I operated a seven day Murray/Coorong safari with my new boat MV "Water Rat". This included a day on the river in our local area, camping up river from our place. We then loaded the boat on to its trailer and travelled down to Jockwar. This bigger boat (20 foot punt with canopy and 50 h.p. four stroke Yamaha) is ideal for lake and Coorong conditions, only drawing 5-6 inches of water, even though it weighs nearly two tonnes.

By using a tarpaulin around the front deck railing, I can considerably raise the freeboard, and it handles two foot waves with no trouble. A couple of days around the lake bought us to the lock on Tauwitcherie Barrage, which is operated to gain access to the Coorong.

After a few false starts through very shallow water, we made the channel and headed off down the Coorong. On this occasion we went within 11 kilometres, of the needles, sometimes getting caught up on the large outcrops of soft "coral". Struck two days of strong winds that made travel not all that pleasant, but the boat handled the rough water extremely well.

We had no luck fishing in this weather, but one of the Coorong fishermen (Eddie Grant) gave us some Coorong mullet, refusing to accept any payment. The next day when we had to load "Water Rat" on the trailer another fisherman Darren Hera-Singh, gave us a lot of help. Over the years, I have always found these fishermen to be very helpful. They live a hard life, but their knowledge of the Coorong is probably second to none, and the government should consult a lot more with them for "Coorong cures". There is a move (as I write) to suspend the fishing licences and a lot of people feel this will be a big mistake.

14

Georgina River – Eyre Creek

In the winter of 1973 I operated a boat safari down that part of the Georgina River known as Eyre Creek – from Lake Muncooney in Queensland, across the border to the flood out region south of the old Alton Downs homestead. This is written up in "Bush Safari".

In the summer of 2001 there were massive monsoonal rains in the gulf country. These caused prolonged flooding in the gulf because the volume of water simply couldn't run into the Gulf of Carpentaria quick enough. The gulf rivers could only drain it so fast, so the effect was a "backing up" of the water inland. The main "back entrance" to this region is the Georgina River, and so a big sustained flood began running down it.

I was soon aware of this, and thought it would provide a good opportunity to operate a boat safari from the channel country around Lake Machattie on the Birdsville/Bedourie Road through to Lake Muncooney. There was quite a lot of channel country between those two locations, but I hoped there would be sufficient water for me to get through.

Regarding the Georgina/Eyre Creek situation, cartographers and geographers have always seemed to have trouble in agreeing where Eyre Creek becomes Eyre Creek and not the Georgina.

Some show this watercourse as being Eyre Creek from the confluence of the Georgina and Hamilton Rivers, but the most favoured local version is that Eyre Creek starts at the confluence of the Georgina and Mulligan – making Eyre Creek a strictly Simpson Desert watercourse. That's the way I see it as well.

So in March of 2001, myself, offsider Luke Talbot–Male and five residents of the south east of South Australia plus a Riverland lady arrived in Birdsville. The weather was hot, as you would expect. We had my usual configuration of the 14' and 12' Stacer punts with 15 h.p. Yamahas. Picked up an Aboriginal mate called Harry Crombie and drove up to the Cuttaburra where I met John Cobb, he is the manager of Glengyle, the biggest station in Queensland, owned by Sid Kidman and Co.

John took us out and pointed out a good entry route into the river, downstream from the channels. We boiled the billy in the shade of a solitary Coolibah tree and had some lunch. Afterwards John headed back to the station and we proceeded across the crabholes of a wide floodplain, eventually locating a suitable launch site.

Next morning we were loaded up and ready to go by 9.30a.m. Harry took off in my Oka for Birdsville, he had a lot of respect for flood waters, but I suspect that he would have liked to have been accompanying us.

We pushed out into the creamy waters and headed off down a temporary new river. It's always a great feeling to start off down a new river.

We soon came to Tommy Donkana Waterhole, then, on to a good navigable channel. It is easy to miss waterholes, but they are usually wider, and deeper than the channel (not always deeper) with larger coolibahs, red gum or river coobah trees, due to the more permanent water. However, it's possible to pass through waterholes without being aware of it. More definite cattle pads are another feature of waterholes.

Pulled up for lunch where a big red sand dune lay across the floodplain, spilling itself into the river. Having a poke about we found some very good Aboriginal stone artefacts, particularly "tules" or scrapers.

After lunch, the channel became narrow, and we had to indulge in a bit of bush bashing to get through. This consisted mainly of Luke and I cutting bush with machetes from the front of our boats. On one occasion I was slashing through coolibah branches when there was a clatter of wings as a duck of some kind flew out of the tree, right in front of me was a nest with eggs!

Into a bit better going and camped that night at Titchery waterhole. This was a lovely area with massive coolibahs, in fact, about the biggest I had seen (in girth) in this part of the world. Stubbie, my jack russell who is a tree climbing dog, had a great time here. Has been a popular Aboriginal camp in the past, evidenced by the number of artefacts and middens in the area. Travelled 38kms that day.

Next morning we travelled through five kilometres of good waterhole then into a narrow channel with lots of bush bashing. In many cases after a quick look, I would swing around, tell the crew to duck their blocks, and charge at the wall of bush. Most times we would get through, but on occasions we ended up in the middle of mass of foliage and had to hack our way to clear water or what passed for it.

About mid morning we were cruising along some nice open channel when I saw a bird I wanted to look at. I had a pair of yellow Minolta binoculars (valued at $400) sitting on a barrel in front of me. As I swung around my thumb caught in the strap and neat as you like I flicked them overboard. I said something I wouldn't normally say in polite company, and there was a stunned silence. But that was that – they had gone forever. Wasn't the first piece of optics I have lost overboard.

As we entered Smith's waterhole, I realised we had something special. Lots of bird sounds over the noise of our outboards, the bulk of which turned out to be strawnecked ibis – hundreds of them. It was a nesting rookery, and I couldn't estimate then numbers. This turned out to be one of the few records of strawnecked ibis nesting in Queensland. Lignum on the south side of the waterhole was crowded with nests as far as the eye could see.

Then I saw a bird that really surprised me; it was a pied heron, a tropical species. Then I saw several more, including some nesting. This turned out, later on, to be an important southerly record for the species. Unusual flooding (this was a big flood) can sometimes provide some unusual bird movements.

Down both sides of the waterhole were unusually large numbers of great egrets, and to cap it off, a spotted harrier flew low over the boat. Unfortunately I was the only real "ornithologist" in the party, and my excitement was not shared. Any "birdo" can relate to this situation.

Into channels again and about midday I got locked into a great tangle of vegetation. Needed fair bit of work and as we hadn't sighted dry land for over an hour, we had lunch in the boats, minus the billy boil. Wouldn't like to have made a habit of it, but it was an "interesting" lunch. At one stage a crow flew into the tree, almost landing on one of the blokes, and I don't know who got the bigger shock!

After working the machetes for about an hour we finally emerged into a boat width channel running entirely through lignums, with hardly a tree in sight. Standing up on my seat it was a sea of lignum on all horizons bar one, where there was a big red sand dune. We travelled in this area for about two hours, before breaking out into a fairly wide channel. Coming across a long sandy island, I pulled up to camp. It was the only dry land we had seen since 11a.m., and I wasn't going to pass it up. I had spent a night in the boats on a Cooper Creek trip in 1974, and wasn't looking for a repeat!

There were a few trees on this island (of about six acres) and enough wood for our fire. Turned out to be a very good camp. Weather had cooled off the last couple of days to around 28 degrees celsius. We had done a hard 18kms that day, heading in the right direction for about two thirds of the time.

Next day we had some good travelling for three kilometres, before trying a channel that I hoped would get me through to Cowarie waterhole. I had to get to that point in order to get out of this bloody great swamp, and through to the junction of the Mulligan.

However, soon ran out of navigable water and returned, I took another channel, travelling okay for seven kilometres before it broke into three channels. I tried all three with plenty of bush bashing and pushing of boats, but they all ran into lignum swamp with un-navigable water.

We had lunch under a big bean tree on a bit of a mud spit, and noticed a snake skin two metres up in the branches. Possibly a bird had carried the snake there. Stubbie climbed up and grabbed it.

There were pig tracks here as well, but we didn't see any. After lunch I did find a channel to Cowarie waterhole, but found it impossible to travel west from there. It was here we realised that we were not going to make it down to Lake Muncooney, which was a big disappointment for all concerned.

Ended up camping in the previous night's camp, after one very frustrating day, heard brolgas that evening.

A few spots of rain, and heard numerous pigs near the camp, giving Stubbie a fairly busy night.

Next morning we began back tracking and it was just as well, there was plenty of cut vegetation to follow. I was able to take a number of short cuts, and saw four dingoes that morning.

Finally got back to the big Meenie sand hill, and only there a while when John Cobb arrived on a motorbike. I had arranged for Harry to bring the Oka and trailer back in from Birdsville and John went and scouted out a good route to get him in, as the flat was pretty wet.

It turned out Harry had trouble with the trailer brakes locking on, and didn't make it that night so we camped under some giant bean trees.

Harry arrived early next morning in time for eggs and bacon, but without the trailer. Three of us went back to sort the trailer out, while Luke took the rest of the party for a boat trip to look for artefacts.

We arrived back with the trailer, loaded up in a hot 40 degrees celsius, and headed for Birdsville. After a feed at the pub, I drove west into the desert, pulling up to camp at the Ten Mile Waterhole at 9.30p.m.

Next day we drove out to Lake Muncooney arriving by 10.30a.m. Making a camp on the East Lake, we did a bit of a boat run over and into the west lake, and up to the point where Eyre Creek was running in.

Back to the camp as it was nearly dark, went back the next day but only got around five kilometres up Eyre Creek before we ran out of navigable water. So we may have had trouble getting through to Muncooney from the North after all. In any case it had been a very worthwhile trip.

Lake Muncooney is a fresh water lake that I have spent a lot of time at over the years. When I owned the Birdsville Pub between 1974 to 1980, we used to run six day trips out there in an old six wheel drive army Studebaker, using a tinny out on the lake. Since it filled for the first time in 1971, I have had many base camps there on my long haul 4WD safaris, and sometimes with the camels.

It is not a permanent lake, but once filled will hold water for several years; there is a West and East Lake. Eyre Creek runs into the top of the West Lake, which is bordered by the big 30m sand dunes of the Simpson Desert. When the west lake fills, it overflows into the East Lake. There are impressive "flat tops" or "breakaways" on the southern and eastern sides of the lakes, giving great views across them.

They can be a "feast" of wildlife, particularly when the East Lake is dry. It is covered with lush green feeds, resembling a Southern dairy paddock. brolgas, bustards (plain turkey) and dingoes are usually well represented, and sometimes emus and red kangaroos, along with myriads of birds.

Sometimes the Eyre Creek floods don't get beyond Lake Muncooney, and it takes a big flood to fill both lakes and then run on down to Goyders Lagoon Swamp, where it joins the waters of the Diamantina River.

Lake Muncooney is incorporated in the Adria Downs Pastoral Lease, owned by the Brook family. Permission should be asked before visiting the Muncooney area.

15

Mitchell River – Cape York Peninsula

By no means a desert river, the Mitchell is the geographical border between Cape York Peninsula and the North Queensland gulf country.

I have known this river since 1969, mainly by crossing the wide bed of sand near Dunbar Station returning from 4x4 vehicle Cape York safaris. During those earlier trips I never dreamt that I would one day travel down it by boat.

That is exactly what we were about to do, as we drove into Charleville to spend the night in the famous Corones Hotel. Famous for its luxury and extravagant décor in the earlier part of the century and particularly during the wool boom of the 50's, when the bush was full of money.

The boat party consisted of my vehicle back up man, Bill Oliver, regular traveller Tony Bomford, his friend Jenny Chapman, very regular traveller Eileen Neeson and Glenda Benness. My wife Patti was also with me, and we met my second boatman, Nick Brooks with his partner and my eldest daughter, Georgi, at the Corones Hotel. Patti and Georgi were to head off back to the east coast while we were away up north.

After a very entertaining evening at the great old pub, we headed off on our separate ways. A couple of days later, I pulled the Oka up in front of the Hurricane Station homestead on the headwaters of the Mitchell. A mate of mine, Terry Martill, was the manager here, and he and his wife Sue were expecting us. We had camped the previous night further up the river at a good camp Terry had put me on to. This cattle station had Japanese owners and I asked Terry about the unusual looking crop we passed as the homestead was approached. It was Hemp, that most excellent of fibres. Apparently it was a trial crop for the Toyota Motor Company who hoped to use it as seat covers for future vehicles to get away from the deadly vinyl that will take forever to break down.

We found this very encouraging. It is one of the great scandals, the fact that hemp is a banned crop in Australia and other parts of the world. Being one of the world's most enduring fibres with a huge range of uses. It is environmentally friendly and not the same plant that produces marijuana, and sooner rather than later the powers that be must get their act together and encourage the cultivation of this wonder plant.

We made camp on the banks of the Mitchell, a couple of kilometres from the station, and an hour later was joined by Richard Hudson, an ABC radio journalist who wanted to travel the first few kilometres with us.

About the same time another old mate, Mick Lund and his girlfriend Carol arrived. I knew Mick from my early trips to Cape York, when he was running is business, Lund's Four Wheel Drive, in Cairns. A Cape York "old hand" and one of the best mechanics in the business, it was good to see him. It was difficult to hear ourselves talk against the background noise of the river, its crystal clear water roaring through scrub and over rocks, on its long journey to the Gulf of Carpentaria. The clear water, and noise were in stark contrast to the near silence and milky water of the desert rivers.

Next morning we packed the two Stacer punts and were finally ready to leave. Terry had told me that from the air there was a clear channel through the Great Dividing Range down to the wider waters on the plains. I knew that several canoe parties had traversed this river, but it had never been traversed by "tinnies". I didn't expect it to be easy, and my crew was under no illusions. They were true adventurers, responsible for their own actions, and keenly anticipating the trip ahead. All were wearing life jackets, at the last moment Mick decided to come with us, and I welcomed his decision, as he had a lot of experience with these Cape York rivers. Bill was going to video our departure, then drive to another spot 10 kilometres down stream where he could get into the river in the Oka, for a bit more "continuity" film and to give Nick his video camera back.

We pushed the boats into the fast flowing water, and then Nick and I had started the 15 h.p. Yamahas and we were off. Richard Hudson was sitting next to me getting some realistic sound effects on his tape recorder, and bouncing questions off me. He wasn't getting very detailed answers, because I had my hands full from the start. We were travelling at a pretty steady rate down a channel some 10 to 15 metres wide, flanked by thick overhanging ti tree, and other larger rain forest species. In a matter of minutes there was a loud bang as I hit a submerged boulder; it pulled us up sharp, allowing a considerable amount of water to cascade into the rear of the boat. It turned out we were only in about 18 inches of water, so I got out and bailed it out. Not a good start.

On our way again, alternating from fast flowing deep water to low water, where we ran around on gravel. We had to be on the lookout for large boulders, both above and under the surface and numerous large snags.

Around a bend and there was a rock bar with shallow water, and banging of boats, but they rode it well. A while later we were bush bashing through ti tree that almost spanned the river.

I was just beginning to think that we had the river's measure when we swept around a tight bend, to be confronted by a log lying right across the river, and about six inches above the water. I gave the motor full power and threw the handle over but my 15h.p. wasn't enough to prevent a sideways collision with the log. What happened next took place in seconds, but it seemed to me as though time had stood still. As my punt hit the log broadside on, my port side went just under the water as the starboard side reared up against the log, aided by the fast flowing current. I found myself pinned between the top canopy rail and a sapling growing in the water. The boat had almost tipped but not quite. My back was hurting and I was totally helpless. It seemed like a long time, but obviously wasn't, the boat moved and I dropped into the water. Our swags and bags were tied in, but I could see other gear heading for the gulf. Then I saw Mick grab Sue by the hair as she emerged from under the water. It transpired that we were only in about four feet of water. Mick was pretty impressed with Sue, because he later said she reared up from under the surface holding her little camera up as though she was taking photos. In actual fact she said she was just trying in vain to keep it dry!

The boat, half full of water, then washed over the log, and headed off downstream with Richard still on board, probably getting a bit too much realism. I could see my camera bag with F5 Nikon and $5,000 worth of gear floating ahead of the boat. Mick and Sue were on the bank, and I could see Nick had pulled in upstream and he was quickly making his way down the bank towards us. The boat momentarily jammed in the fork of a Ti Tree, and I yelled to Richard to make it fast with a rope. This he quickly did, and the thought flashed through my mind that he might have been wasted with the ABC.

I then began swimming after my beloved F5, cursing to myself as I realised my hat was missing, nothing I hate worse than losing a hat. Then to my amazement the bloody thing passed by me. I lunged at it, got it and jammed it on my head. I hoped it was a good omen. Maybe it was, because my camera bag caught up in a tree, and I managed to get it – otherwise I doubt I could have retrieved it. I waded into shore and headed back to the "scene".

With considerable difficulty we managed to tow my boat with Nick's to the opposite bank. I rang the station on my satellite phone and told Terry what had happened, and that I would keep him posted as it was a very difficult place to get into by vehicle.

In the meantime, Bill had been waiting for us 10 kilometres downstream. He was sitting on the bank contemplating the river when a loaf of bread floated past him. He was digesting this (metaphorically) when it was followed by a container of boat fuel and a dozen stubbies. It was then he realised we weren't having a very good day, and quickly began walking up the river towards us, arriving at our camp an hour later.

By this time we had unrolled swags and spread everything wet out to dry. Mick and Nick had pulled the outboard down from my boat, as it had been underwater. Within an hour Mick had it running sweetly, which was a big step in the right direction.

My camera and gear looked like being a write off, and although insured it was a big blow. Most people hadn't lost too much, although Sue's camera was not functioning and Richard's recorder had been under. Tony said he had lost a much-valued old toilet bag. My main loss was four 20 litre containers of boat fuel, several cartons and one polythene tub of stores, long handled shovel, machete etc. – things that weren't tied down.

Nick and I went for a bit of cruise downstream, and managed to retrieve two items – a boiled fruit cake, and would you believe, Tony's toilet bag, washed up against some debris. We went back to camp and I noticed Tony was sitting in his camp sorting his clothes. I wandered over and dropped his bag in front of him. His day was made!

The lines were in and we caught a couple of nice sized black bream for the evening meal. All our gear was dry by sun down, and we camped there for the night. Next morning we packed the boats, and travelled very carefully about four kilometres downstream to the Oka, and landed. Soon after Terry, Sue and Carol arrived in Terry's Toyota.

Reluctantly I had decided to pull the boat out, we may have managed to get through, but I wasn't prepared to put the people at risk even though they would have gone. My intention was to drive back to Mareeba to replace our stores and fuel, and then drive down to Gamboola Station which was out of the ranges.

We spent two pleasant days in the quarters at Hurricane, waiting for some Oka parts and straightening out the framework on my boat which had been badly twisted. People fished and swam in the river, and on the second day we all went out with Terry and had a picnic lunch on the King George River, part of which was on the Hurricane run. Mick, Terry, Bill and I also visited a gold mine to try and find a certain sized washer for the Oka, and were much impressed by a pet pig that seemed to run the show. It was on a sticky wicket having recently eaten the manager's good looking girlfriends' credit cards and mobile phone! She had given him an ultimatum – either her or the pig, so the pig was getting his marching orders. The manager intended giving it to a mate.

Saying goodbye to the hospitable Hurricane crew, we headed off to Mareeba, where we replenished our gear. In the afternoon we drove through the rich Atherton

Tableland, through the bush covered ranges around Chillagoe, finally arriving at Gamboola Station and the Mitchell just after dark. We cooked a feed and rolled out the swags, anticipating the continuation of our journey.

It was a different river that met our eyes next morning. Around a 100 metres wide the water running about six inches over a concrete causeway. We put the boats in, loaded up, and making arrangements with Bill for a down river rendezvous, we once again headed off. Shallow water with a bit of pushing for 10 minutes before good travelling.

We were now in saltwater crocodile territory, and had to take the appropriate precautions with indiscriminate swimming being the main casualty.

It is a very beautiful river, a different beauty compared to the desert rivers with which I am so familiar. Blue water, instead of brown and the trees among the luxuriant vegetation. Bird life was much in evidence, with dollar birds and red backed sea eagles (brahminy kite) being of interest.

The river was taking on a definite pattern with large sweeping regular bends. On most of these we would have to try and find the best way through large sand and gravel bars. Mick was good at this perching up on the back of the steel frame. But on many occasions we would run out of water. This often meant us blokes out pushing, while Nick would sit back and see how we got on, then sometimes taking an alternate route. We kept a good look out for salties and I kept my rifle handy when we were out pushing. All of a sudden we would get back into water metres deep, on one occasion Glenda was out as well, pushing up the front, when she suddenly walked into deep water. She is no ballerina and I had to grab her by the hair to pull her in. However she fairly flew back over the side, the thought of lurking salties adding extra incentive.

The many hours of churning through gravel was taking its toll on our props with mine being reduced by almost a third in diameter. I was pretty worried about getting stranded on one of these bars with hundreds of metres of deep water, but we always managed to make it through, and certainly getting our daily exercise.

Eileen who weighed about as much as a feather would just continue to read her ever-present book, completely unflappable in any situation. She had been on so many wild trips over the years, that she had an absolute blind faith in me. Now that is pretty scary.

All the time, Nick was busy, not only operating his boat, but taking video of our trip.

Then we came across the first of the major rock bars. They are definitely not designed for tinnies, but I had no alternative but to have a go at them. Pulling the boats out in most places wasn't an option, as it was not feasible to get a vehicle in. I had a good look at the first one, picked a spot and made for it. Nick sat back a bit and ran the video. We were suddenly into it with much movement and banging against rock. The Stacer is of such solid construction I wasn't concerned about holing it; my main fear was being caught in rock, and the then taking water over the rear of the boat. In a few seconds we fishtailed through the turbulent water and into safe water again. It was a bit of an adrenalin rush, and Nick followed the same route without incident.

After 20 kilometres, we had lunch on a nice sandy beach, watching a Jabiru go about its business and a nice white bellied sea eagle cruise by. After lunch another similar rock bar, which we came through without difficulty except a bit of wear and tear on the nervous system.

About 4p.m. we came to the junction of the Lynd River, where Bill was waiting for us, and we made camp with him having travelled 45 kilometres for the day.

Soon after we left next morning, we came to another rock bar; we went through but took in a bit of water. Then an hour later the biggest rock bar yet. I considered taking the passengers out, but decided that with their life jackets on they were okay with the boats. I held my breath and headed through a bit of a gap, with a bang we stopped, the prop caught on a rock. The water came within inches of the back of our boat, but not a lot came in. I was able to wrench the motor up, freeing the prop, and nearly went over the back myself as the boat shot forward through 50 metres of foaming water to safety. I was beginning to long for the desert rivers. Nick came through holding his motor up.

A few kilometres further on we came to the New Hugh's Crossing, and met up with Bill again, he was relieved to see us because the station owner had assured him that there was no way "tinnies" could make it down that last section of river. I knew one thing – I wouldn't be repeating the process!

While we were pulling into the crossing, my motor cut out and wouldn't start, so Nick towed me in while Mick was looking at the motor, a grader pulled up on the other side of the river and entered the water. It crossed over through about a metre and half of water. We reckoned that if we had seen it half way across the river as we approached in the boats, our eyes might have widened somewhat. It was Colin Hughes from Rum Duff Station nearby, who Mick knew and his eyes widened a bit when he heard where we had come from. He graded the approaches to the crossing while we boiled the billy. Trouble with the motor turned out to be a blocked jet in the carby.

We pulled away after a couple of hours, soon after spotting a 14 foot croc on a sandbar, but he slid into the river before we could approach too closely. Also saw a couple of five foot Water Monitors.

After making 35 kilometres for the day, I found a nice camp on natural "lawn" about 30 feet above the river.

Next morning away about 8.30a.m., encountering the usual sand and gravel bars. Saw a white bellied sea eagle and a few kilometres further on found two adult birds on a nest in a dead eucalypt. Couldn't see if they had eggs or small chicks. Managed to get quite close before they flew off. Also saw a brush turkey 15 metres up in the branches of a tree.

At lunchtime we inspected the deadly "rubber vine" the exotic that has been slowly strangling a lot of bush in the gulf country. In places it was so thick that there was no way you would force your way through with a vehicle. Its pliable rubbery tentacles are very hard to cut through as well.

The good news is they have found a cure for it and the problem is slowly being pegged back.

A funny thing happened that day concerning wild pigs. Nick had been filming constantly, and in the interests of a possible documentary sometime down the track, I was after some footage of myself shooting a pig. We hadn't managed to shoot any pigs so far, not having seen a great many, although we often heard them near our camps at night. We had one big walk off the river to some inland lagoons, but couldn't get close enough for a good shot with my .375 Winchester Carbine. So I said to Nick that we might have to indulge in a bit of "artistic licence" and simulate a shooting, We could fill in the dead pig art at another location. Typical film makers "trickery"! So that afternoon we landed near a bit of gallery rainforest, with a lot of thick high grass and other ground cover. I walked along with the rifle, my body language looking like I was "on" to pigs, with Nick walking behind filming. Suddenly I raised the rifle to my shoulder and fired at the base of a large tree, some 30 metres distant. Next thing, a large boar sprang up from the other side of the tree and ran off. I fired once more, but couldn't get a good bead on it. Nick got it all on film then lay down on the ground laughing his head off; all we need now is the dead pig.

That night we camped on a grassy sand hill high above the river. Nick went off in his boat and half an hour later, returned with an eight pound and three pound barramundi for our dinner, the second ones for the trip.

Next day we headed on, looking for the mouth of the Palmer River. I wanted to camp early there because I had a reliable report of an 18 foot croc that lived in the area. I intended camping up on the bank above the mouth on the off chance of spotting it. However, we missed the mouth as we were trapped by a sand bank on the far side and it wasn't visible. I ended up camping about a kilometre downstream on the same side, near some rocky outcrops and plenty of snags – good barramundi country. Mick soon caught an eight pounder, and let him go. Bit early he reckoned. A few hours later I hooked a really big one on a handline; it jumped out of the water, and bit through the line! I'm only glad there were a couple of witnesses. Later still Nick caught a six pounder that would do for our meal.

Later still Nick managed to get some good video of a dingo waking along a flat at the back of the river in some rough country. Next thing a wild boar sprang out of the bush and chased it for a few metres. The pig took off but the dingo kept wandering around for 10 minutes, quite close to Nick.

The last day was pleasant and uneventful, and that evening we had one of our most idyllic camps. Up on a steep bank under palms and overlooking colourful sandbars on the other side of the inlet where we were camped. Beautiful reflections last light as Nick returned in his boat with his regular "barra" contribution.

Next morning, after a couple of hours travel we arrived at the Dunbar Crossing, and there was Bill with the Oka and trailer. The end of our trip, there was no time to get down to the Aboriginal community of Kowanyuma, but it didn't matter. This had been a "one off" and a very worthwhile one at that. We had travelled a distance of around 120 kilometres. The last thing Nick filmed, was my outboard prop, the gravel had reduced it to half its original size, with practically no fins left on it.

16

Aboard the Water Rat

In 2002 I purchased a six metre aluminium punt from Queensland, and had it transported down to Waikerie Engineering in Waikerie. Phil Bishop rebuilt it from the hull up, giving it a very robust aluminium framework and "roof rack" on top, heavy duty canvas and a 50 h.p. four stroke Yamaha motor more or less completed the job. The hull is constructed of double sided aluminium builder's "planks". Despite the weight it only draws five inches of water when empty, and only around nine inches when fully laden giving access to a lot of shallow water areas.

I required this boat for summer safaris on the Murray River, and winter safaris on the tropical rivers.

That first summer I operated a number of short trips from the camel farm, as well as a seven day Murray River/Coorong safari, and three and six day Murray River trips. The three day finished at Barmera on Lake Bonney, and the six day went on and included the Lindsay Creek area in Victoria. The boat worked very well, and now I operate mostly two and a half hour, one, three and six day trips in the summer.

THE VICTORIA RIVER

This is one of the north's "wild rivers" and had long been of interest to me. The navigable section (nearly 200kms) from Timber Creek to the coast runs through a lot of remote wilderness – large cattle stations on the western side, and the massive Bradshaw Army Reserve on the eastern side.

I thought there was scope for the extended boat camping safaris on some of the tropical rivers, nobody else was doing it.

In May 2003, I set off from home, towing the Water Rat behind the Oka. A mate, Greg Pettman, was coming with me for the ride to Timber Creek, and then flying back from there. I had just the one lady (Ann Entick) for the trip, as there were a couple of late cancellations. My offsider, Darren Wallace, would meet me in Katherine.

We had an uneventful trip up, arriving in Katherine four days later and picking up Ann and Darren. Late that evening we arrived at Timber Creek, and rolled the swags out on a reserve near the town.

Early next morning it was apparent that Greg had put in a bad night suffering severe stomach pains. We looked up Neville Foggarty at his garage, and he sent us down to his wife Meredith who was the local nursing sister. To cut a long story short, Greg jumped on a coach to Darwin, and has a lot to thank Meredith for, her accurate diagnosis of kidney stones was correct.

The local tour boat operator, Geoff Pike and Neville Foggarty were very helpful with information. I had experience with the high tides of the N.W. tropics in other areas, and they certainly applied to the Victoria. We put the boat in at the local boat ramp, and Neville picked up the Oka and trailer to look after while we were away.

About 11.30a.m. we headed off upstream under the new army bridge, and pulled up for lunch a kilometre further on. We boiled the billy up on the bank, having to push our way through two metre high marshmallow or similar. This plant covers large areas on the banks of this river. After lunch we motored about seven kilometres to a good campsite, a little further up a large rock bar more or less defined the end of any navigable water. It was a good camp. Fairly steep sandy banks ran down to a little inlet some 20 metres or so. I tied the Water Rat in the inlet to some river gums, and an animal pad gave us reasonable access up on to the bank with our gear. There were nice views through the timber of big red bluffs, with the river looking remarkably blue.

Next morning we got going about 8a.m. and headed down river under the bridge and past the boat ramp where a few people were fishing. We stopped a couple of times to fish, but without any success and on another occasion did a short walk up along some interesting breakaways. I had Stubbie with me, and was very aware of the crocodile danger when we were getting on and off of the boat. Crocs love eating dogs.

I pulled into a camp on the western bank at around 4p.m., and tied up with heavy nylon rope to two trees, with the bow of the Water Rat into shore. Being very conscious of the high rise and fall of the tide in this area, I made sure with the depth finder that there was deep water under the boat, as I know the tide would fall and rise again that night. We carried our gear some 12 metres up a shelving clear bank. There were plenty of agile wallabies and Stubbie had a couple of chases to get his exercise for the day, without any hope of catching them. I rolled my swag out right on the edge of the bank, so that I could check on the boat through the night. If I sat up in my swag I could see the boat. I was close to the fire with the extra wood put on to deter the unlikely interest of a croc. Stubbie was in the bottom of my swag, and my .375 rifle was next to me. As I drifted off to sleep, a full moon was spreading diluted light through the gums. I had no idea that tomorrow was going to be a day I would remember a long time for all the wrong reasons. On three or four occasions through the night I woke up and checked that all was okay with the boat, and then I must have fallen into a deep sleep, because I was awakened by a large metallic rattling noise. I sat up in my swag, and the sight that presented itself made me go cold inside. All I could see of the Water Rat was the foredeck and part of the front part of the canvas roof cover. It had sunk at its mooring. I yelled out to Darren, making sure I received an answer and ran down the bank. The moon was still well up and I could see quite well. Inside the boat I could see gear floating, some of it (vegetables) already floating down river on the outgoing tide. The fridge was floating, held only by the power cable, I hesitated for a few seconds. We had been told by locals that there was a 16 foot croc resident diagonally opposite our camp. That was definitely on my mind, but I knew that if I didn't do something straight away, we would have no gear left and that would definitely be the end of the trip – if it wasn't already over. As Darren came down the bank, I jumped onto the front of the Rat, throwing gear out to Darren. Then I swam into the interior under the roof for more gear. I pulled the plug out of the fridge and floated that out to Darren.

Darren then came into the front of the boat and together we cleared the rest of the gear. I had been in there for less than five minutes, but it seemed like a lot longer. We had lost mostly food as far as I could see.

There was nothing else we could do before daylight, so went back into the swag, laying there with sleep out of the question. It was fortunate that my ropes were heavy duty enough. There was a lot of weight on them, but they hadn't looked like breaking. If they had, the boat would have probably been a goner. As it was, maybe I could get out this predicament as I was only about 30kms from Timber Creek; I hoped it might be possible to get my Oka into this camp, with winching a possibility. When Ann got up, I told her there wasn't any hurry this morning – we wouldn't be getting away early! She had slept through the early hour's drama, and I could see no point in waking her.

At around 7a.m. I rang Neville Foggarty on my sat phone, and filled him in on events. He said that he would be able to get the Oka into the location, another 10kms down river and it would have been out of the question. He said he would be down in a couple of hours. I then rang Geoff the tour boat operator, and arranged for him to come down in his big boat, after that we had a lazy breakfast waiting for the boys, and trying to work out what had happened.

Geoff arrived first in the boat, and 20 minutes later I could hear the Oka coming through the bush. I headed out to show Neville where we were as the bush was pretty thick – mainly gum saplings.

We boiled the billy, and worked out a plan of attack. I started off by driving the Oka in 4WD low range bottom up to a stout river gum near the top of the bank, above the boat. We ran the winch cable down to the Water Rat and attached to the big lug on the front of the hull, after first running the cable through a "snatch block", that is a pulley firmly attached to a point out to one side of the direct pull. This gives twice the pulling power, and in this case it was well justified, with water inside the boat it was one hell of a weight to pull out of the river. We started the motor and began winching. The tree did a bit of shuddering but didn't look like moving. Slowly the Water Rat began to emerge from the river, some minutes later the stern was above the water allowing us to get in and start bucketing water out. When we had cleared most of it Geoff moved his boat up, and we attached a rope to the bow of my boat. It wasn't much trouble to slew the Rat around so that it was floating parallel to the bank. Great relief.

Initially I felt a bit of an idiot because it looked like it was my inexperience that had caused the sinking. It helped a little bit when both Neville and Geoff said that it was quite common for this to happen to boats on this river, but not much. I had to wait until later that afternoon to find out all the facts of the matter.

Neville had pulled both Yamaha motors down, and soon had those running smoothly; the fridge however, needed a major operation when I returned home. So it was decided that Geoff would drop me some ice along with other stores when he did his daily tour run down to the Angalarri River the following day. They headed off in the Oka and boat, and we spent the rest of the day getting sorted out.

We had worked out what caused the sinking. When I had moored the boat I was careful that there was plenty of water underneath. I tied up leaving plenty of slack when the tide dropped; the bow was suspended except that the outlet hole for the bilge pumps was just below the water, which shouldn't be a problem. However, that afternoon Darren was doing something in the rear of the boat, and noticed water inside, on further inspection, he saw that water was actually siphoning into the boat from through the bilge pump (ref. Darren Wallace).

Our luck was in, because if that hadn't been noticed we may possibly have had a repeat performance. It just emphasised some of the ever present hazards on these tropical rivers with a big rise and fall of tide. I subsequently stopped mooring to the bank of a night, and after setting up camp, I would anchor off shore, come into camp in the Avon inflatable. When it was time to roll the swag, either myself or my offsider would camp on the boat. A much safer arrangement.

We spent all next morning cleaning the boat out and preparing to continue our trip. We actually retrieved most of our tucker on the incoming tide. A butternut pumpkin, numerous oranges and a pineapple presented themselves for service, and were plucked out of the river using the dinghy. All our meat was okay as it was in the fridge.

After an early lunch we headed off downstream arriving at the Angalarri River mouth an hour or so before dark. This tributary enters from the east side, a dramatic spot with the big flat top Ranges providing an impressive backdrop. It drains some of the Bradshaw Army Reserve, and we had glimpsed the old Bradshaw homestead through the bush. It's only occupant now is a caretaker employed by the army. There were numerous notices warning that it was an offence to enter Bradshaw.

On the west side the land sloped gently down to the river, providing good campsites. We moored and carried camp gear 70 metres or so back to the tree line and set up camp. A good evening was had.

We spent the next couple of days here doing some walks inland. Not far in was a shallow lagoon with good birdlife. I took good long lens shots of a wedge tailed eagle, and red backed wrens were numerous. We had been on the lookout for the threatened gouldian finches but with no sightings so far. Agile wallabies were as numerous on this river as I had ever seen them, and Stubbie was wearing himself out chasing them.

We went up the Angalarri a few kilometres before a rock bar prevented further travel. Did a bit of fishing but no luck. There were two moored boats here, a homemade houseboat belonging to Neville Foggarty – his "escape" when things got too hectic in Timber Creek. Plus a pontoon with a shed, a dining barge for the tour boat from Timber Creek.

We continued on downstream, setting up a camp on sandy Island. Darren and I explored this small island covered in very thick tropical grass and eucalyptus down one end. A lot of effort for not much reward had to be careful we didn't stumble on crocs near the river. It provided a good camp that evening, with a couple of fair sized crocs floating on top of coloured water as the sun set with numerous water birds flying past – including a flock of about 40 Glossy Ibis.

We did a run down river next morning for 20kms before returning to camp. No fish, and in the afternoon we passed Max, the fishing guide, and he said not much was biting at the moment.

The next few days were spent cruising slowly back up river viewing and filming numerous "salties" sunning themselves on the muddy banks during the heat of the day. The biggest around 12 feet.

Duly arriving back at the boat ramp, we loaded the boat and headed South.

17

Victoria River – Second Trip

In May 2004, we set off down the Victoria again with five of us on board. Nick Brooks, was offsiding again and the party consisted of an old mate of mine Dick Vincent, who used to own stations in WA and a couple of friends of his, all very keen fishermen.

The day was overcast, in fact we hardly saw the sun for 10 days, and it turned out to be one of the wettest Mays on record. Fortunately most of the rain on our trip fell at night; there had been a lot of rain earlier in the month, unusual in the tropics.

We headed upstream under the army bridge, having lunch and doing some fishing. Then turned around and back down past the Timber Creek boat ramp. We camped reasonably early on high banks and Nick headed over the other side in the Avon to try for a fish. Within half an hour he gave a shout and looking over we saw him holding up a large barramundi. It turned out to be nearly 30 pounds and made a delicious meal that night. I did a silly thing and trod on a hot coal in bare feet when I was cooking. Copped a reasonably nasty burn on the bottom of the foot. We made a big dressing so that I could hobble around. It caused me a lot of inconvenience for four or five days.

Headed down to the Angalarri River and set up another camp. Spent a day fishing in the area. No barras, but plenty of good size catfish.

The weather was looking very much like rain as we headed down stream from the Angalarri, so I pulled into a likely looking camp five kilometres down stream from Green Island. The bank tapered down to a little mangrove gutter, which provided a good mooring and landing. We set up camp with tents on top of the three metre bank and began collecting a good supply of wood. Got a big fire going, and were just able to finish our meal when it began raining lightly.

I anchored the boat about 20 metres off shore and camped on the boat. This was regular practice now after the sinking episode. I would keep the Avon inflatable with me.

It rained quite steadily through the night and indeed on and off the next day. Spent most of the day in camp boiling the billy numerous times.

We spent two nights here and as we were about to leave next morning, found that my main anchor had come off. We spent a couple of hours trawling for it, but no luck. Headed down river reaching the Baines River about midday. This is a very scenic area with large flat topped mountain ranges all around. There is a large bluff overlooking the southern side of the mouth, very colourful with varied vegetation. We landed on a nice beach at the foot of it and we had a walk inland. I climbed half way up the hill and had a good view.

We had lunch here and Dick gave a yell and a wave from where he had walked along the beach. We joined him and he said, "Here's our new anchor!" He'd found a large irregularly shaped rock that was possible to put a wire twitch on. We manhandled it over to the boat and loaded it on to the foredeck, wired it up and attached the anchor chain to it. We had an anchor.

That afternoon we motored steadily downstream and reached the mouth of the Bulloo River by 4p.m. This river has a false mouth we found out later, and we tried unsuccessfully for an hour to get in, but low water kept beating us. In the end we gave it away and reluctantly turned back up river looking for a camp.

The Victoria River has never been officially charted and caution needs to be exercised all the time. Some fisherman we met on a small trawler told us about a whirlpool down closer to the mouth. There are a number of islands as well, but we weren't going to see them this trip.

A few kilometres up from the Bulloo we saw a possible campsite with only an hour of light left. There was a flat section of rock an acre or so in area jutting out into the river. We were able to tie up here and carry our camp across the rock and up on to a rise. Made camp next to a couple of pandanus palms, then Nick and I went back and anchored the Water Rat out from the rocks.

The rock anchor worked well and I also had a smaller rear anchor. We came back in the rubber duck and had a meal. We were able to collect plenty of wood because we were a bit vulnerable to crocs here. Made sure everyone slept close to the fire. Nick headed back to spend the night on the Water Rat.

Next morning we visited a very interesting permanent campsite. A few days back we met an old couple from Timber Creek heading back from their camp. They told us to use it if we wished. They also told us about a particular notorious croc down there and an incident that occurred a week before. A fishing guide from Timber Creek was fishing with a couple of European clients when the big croc surfaced behind their tinny. It gave a roar and blew water out the top of its head! The guide belted it on the head with his rod and it submerged, but the clients had had enough, and demanded to be taken back to Timber Creek. The theory is that it had a bullet hole in the top of its head that made it a bit "cranky"! The couple told me where it hung out and I was keen to get a look at it – from the Water Rat, not the rubber duck.

We arrived at the camp, in a very attractive setting. There is a large boabab tree (bottle tree) with a huge white bellied sea eagle's nest in it. The couple have made pets of them. Their small hut built out of mostly driftwood is located only metres from the base of the tree. We had our lunch in their "barbecue area" seeing a bit of the sea eagles.

That afternoon I went across to the mangrove creek nearby, and went up a couple of kilometres hoping to see the croc, but no go. We did some fishing at the mouth, and got some nice catfish for dinner.

Headed up to the Bulloo River and set up a tricky little camp at the base of the bluff, had to anchor the Water Rat and bring in gear with the Avon making several trips, then carry it across an area of large rocks to a little beach. Just enough area to light a fire and put the table. Too dangerous to camp because of crocs, so I found a few little "possies" up the steep slopes of the bluff for swags to be rolled out, certainly a spectacular spot, but lots of effort required.

I camped on the boat that night didn't get a lot of sleep due to a fair wind blowing against incoming tide, and worrying about anchor dragging. I rigged up a couple of bells so they would fall down on to the deck and make a racket if the boat started to drift, but the anchor held and I was glad to head in for breakfast next morning.

The morning's tide was particularly strong and was causing the Water Rat to drag the anchor. A wind was also blowing against the tide and it was a difficult transfer back to camp. Nick started the motor and left the boat idling into the wind, which stopped the anchor drag. It took us about 20 minutes shuttling between the camp and boat to get all gear and people aboard, but was finally completed. It took four of us to pull up the anchor and get it stowed on the deck.

We motored back to our "wet camp" and were surprised to see our big fire was still smouldering. Must have been some really good timber in there somewhere. We tied up and set up camp again before having lunch.

That afternoon we went over to a channel that went around the east side of Sandy Island, and started fishing, mostly from the boat, but I also landed Dick and Nick on a sand spit to fish. Keeping an eye open for crocs. Managed to get a few catfish, enough for a feed. The sea eagles were active, putting on their usual floor show.

This was the river that Rod Ansell had travellers down on a fishing expedition with his two Bull Terrier pups. Something "large" had up-ended his larger boat down near the mouth and he had managed to get himself and pups (one suffered a broken leg) into his towed dinghy. His swag, rifle, ammo and limited food with very little water was aboard. He drifted for several days out of the Victoria Mouth, and luckily into the mouth of the Fitzmaurice River. He travelled on the incoming tide up that river to the fresh water. Rock bars prevented further travel and he spent many weeks surviving there, living in a tree platform to, keep away from the crocs, and hunting wild cattle. This story and his eventual rescue are told in his book "To Fight the Wild". His later shoot out with police is a sad and tragic ending to one of Australia's latter day bushmen.

Our last day took us back past the Angalarri River, where we spent a couple of hours fishing. We caught a couple of nice jewfish here. The sea eagles were still with us and I got some good shots of them snatching fish heads and entrails from in front of our noses.

18

Obituary to Stubbie

We headed back to Timber Creek, ending another trip on this exciting river.

In September 2004, Patti and I were away on an ornithological charter, and as was sometimes the case, had left Stubbie and his mother ("Bigger") at home. They had the run of the large backyard and shed, with neighbours calling in daily to feed them.

Ten days into the trip, I had a message from the neighbours saying that Stubbie was missing, and had been since day five, we were devastated, and my first thought was that he had fallen victim to a brown snake. We had lost two other jack russell's to brown snakes.

When we duly arrived home, I scoured the cliffs and all his favourite haunts, looking for his body. Soon after we arrived home, we learnt that the neighbours had found a gate open. This in itself wouldn't have been a problem. Both dogs would have simply have gone off along the cliffs looking for the odd rabbit, like they often did, before returning. None of the neighbours would have left it open, so I soon began to realise that he had been stolen.

I had mixed emotions about that. The first one was outrage one of the lowest acts in the bush is to steal someone's dog, on a parallel with kidnapping your kids, because your dog is very much a part of your family. Especially when you live in isolated circumstances.

The positive aspect was that "he's still out there" and maybe I can get him back, especially in a state like South Australia. Of all the states, SA is more like a big country club than any other, especially in the country, you only have to talk to some stranger, and after a few minutes of conversation you would usually discover mutual acquaintances.

I thought that if I was going to do something, I would have to throw in every possible resource at my disposal.

First I contacted a journalist friend at The Advertiser, and no doubt helped by the fact that I had been around for a long time, and more particularly, that Stubbie had a pretty high profile for a dog. Anyway, they ran a small article with a photograph of Stubbie, for which I was very grateful.

I had offered a substantial reward for information leading to his recovery, and received half a dozen very positive reports that he had been seen (I don't think the reward had much to do with people ringing up). The locations were Strathalbyn, Mannum, Morgan and up river in NSW at Boundary Bend.

In the meantime, I had placed an ad in our local paper (with picture) and had two radio interviews. After the reports of sightings I phoned dozens of people in the areas – in fact I spent so much time on the phone I became hoarse for days. I kept walking around the cliffs locally, and drove around as well.

Its now a month since he disappeared and still no luck, I realise that it will be a very long shot if I get him back, but I have always played long shots, sometimes with success. I keep thinking of "Bundy Rum", my white bull terrier on Kangaroo Island who returned after living in the bush for three months.

There are just two things I will recount regarding Stubbie, that I didn't mention in my chapter on dogs.

The first was when I was pulled up in front of Johnny Teague's service station in Hawker, Stubbie was sitting up in the driving seat of my Oka, and a young German girl backpacker walked over from her bus to look at Stubbie. As I walked up she said, "That little dog should be in films", and I knew what she meant.

The other occasion was early this year when I was doing a boat safari up the Murray. I was sitting up in my swag about to get up one morning. Stubbie came out from the bottom of my swag. A few days before he had injured his nearside hind leg and was favouring it a bit. He walked over to a small branch as he cocked his leg he immediately fell over, no sooner had he hit the ground than he sprang up again, looking very surprised. I cracked up laughing, it was the funniest thing to see one of the most agile dogs so compromised, it happened in a split second and I still laugh when I think of it.

Stubbie is nearly seven years old, a fairly long life for a "working" jack russell, in his case that would just about equate to 70 years of living. He was/is special and I haven't given up on him yet. This can be a "temporary obituary", very easily cancelled or put on hold, should I get the little bloke back.

About the Author

Rex Ellis was born in 1942 and lives with his wife, Patti, at their Murray River camel farm. Their rammed earth and native timber house is surrounded by old growth Mallee scrub and located on colourful cliffs overlooking the River Murray. From this semi desert base he operates short summer safaris by camel, boat or 4WD vehicle, and longer safaris throughout the outback of Australia in the winter.After jackerooing and overseeing on sheep stations for six years, he began his safari business in 1965, operating in many 'non tourist' areas.

In 1971 he led the first party of tourists to cross the Simpson Desert and subsequent trips to other deserts and tropical regions, such as; Cape York Peninsula, The Gulf Country and the Kimberley region. His regular 4WD 'bread and butter' trips were to the Nullarbor /Great Victoria Desert and Birdsville/Strzelecki Tracks, and Flinders Ranges. He purchased the Birdsville Pub in 1973, and for six years used it as a base for trips into the Simpson Desert. Inland boat safaris became a specialty of his , after making the first and only crossing of Lake Eyre by boat during the 1974 floods. Since then he has followed most of the inland's flooding rivers and continues to do so. In 1976 he pioneered long haul desert camel expeditions and has crossed all of the Australian deserts.

This continues along with regular Flinders Ranges Treks. All of his itineraries are nature based. The four books he has written describe many of these journeys. His first book *Bush Safari*, details his earliest and more unusual trips by vehicle, boat, and camel. *Mulga Madness* includes several unusual safaris, but its main focus is on hilarious incidents on the sleep stations, bush towns and safaris, as well as some outrageous practical jokes. *Outback By Camel*, gives a comprehensive account of contemporary travel in the outback of Australia. He has almost completed his fifth book, *Boats In The Desert*.

In between times he writes his books, plants native trees, and pursues his interest in wildlife, in particular, birds.

Books by

Rex Ellis

Ten Thousand Campfires

Boats in the Desert

Mulga Madness

Mopokes and Mirages